Ecstatic Speech

Expressions of True Nonduality

Reviews and endorsements for Jason Shulman's work

About *The Instruction Manual for Receiving God:*

"A Dharma teacher and Kabbalist, Jason Shulman has succeeded in creating a down-to-earth guide which makes the quest to find God into a realizable possibility."

> — Deepak Chopra, M.D., author of *Life After Death: The Burden of Proof*

"Beautiful lessons and brilliant insights on the divine nature of humanity and how we connect with God and ourselves. Enlightening and inspirational."

> — Stephen R. Covey, author, *The 7 Habits of Highly Effective People* and *The 8th Habit: From Effectiveness to Greatness*

"The Instruction Manual for Receiving God contains exactly the type of common sense wisdom required for a person to live a good old-fashioned grounded life in a society that encourages us to do things faster while multi-tasking. This book is a magnificent breath of tranquil air."

> — Caroline Myss, author of *Anatomy of the Spirit* and *Sacred Contracts*

"Jason Shulman offers us a profoundly simple guide to the obviousness of awakening to our deepest Self. Lucid, contemporary, and most of all kind, this is a beautiful book which goes to the very heart of the human condition, by encouraging us to embrace both the impersonal oneness of all things and the richness of the personal life."

> — Timothy Freke, author of *Lucid Living*

"A beautiful book that brings the western spiritual tradition into our modern world. It's deep, thoughtful, exciting, and we can use it to find out how we live when we are fully human."

— John Tarrant, author of *Bring Me the Rhinoceros*

About *Kabbalistic Healing: A Path to an Awakened Soul:*

"Jason Shulman is a true adept of the inner teachings. He offers a very sophisticated and dynamic account of what happens between the Kabbalah and the great, luminous transparency. To engage with Jason Shulman's mind is to enter into the reality where true healing can occur."

— Rabbi Zalman Schachter-Shalomi, Founder of the Jewish Renewal Movement

"This lucid book of deep healing is a brilliant contribution to the spiritual literature bridging Eastern and Western thought. Shulman's bigger view unifies seeking and being-there, path and goal, transcendence and immanence, with the joy of a true master."

— Lama Surya Das, founder of the Dzogchen Center and author of *Awakening the Buddha Within*

"Jason Shulman brilliantly integrates a deep psychological component with a profound understanding of the non-dual, absolute unity of the Divine Nature in a way that raises the reader's soul to the highest potential of awareness. While traditional teachings tend to demean the ego-self, Shulman shows us the importance of our gift of self-awareness and how to come to peace with ourselves. Thus he leads readers to evoke a healing from our sense of fractured separation into a wholeness of being that has compassion for who we are and what we are. This is a must-read for anyone who wishes to learn the essence of kabbalistic teachings in the hands of a master of spiritual and psychological development."

— Rabbi David A. Cooper, author of *God Is a Verb*

"Here is once and future wisdom as we meet the Jewish mystical tradition in its revelatory mapping of the nature of reality. Here too are practices that bring the reader closer to the nondual state of consciousness and awareness of the integral relationship between all things. Taken seriously, this profound work can only charge the spirit as it illumines the mind and heart."

— Jean Houston, PH.D., author of *Jump Time: Shaping Your Future in a World of Radical Change*

"*Kabbalistic Healing* is a great book about discovering wisdom within each of us. At a time when everyone in contemporary society is experiencing an information glut, what's missing is a deeper understanding of life. Jason Shulman provides the reader with wisdom and insight for life's journey."

— Stephan Rechtschaffen, cofounder of the Omega Institute for Holistic Studies, and creator and director of Blue Spirit Costa Rica.

"Jason Shulman is a sincere, authentic practitioner of Kabbalah. The fruit of much inner work, the masterful teachings in this book resonate and come alive because he has truly experienced this wisdom from deep inside."

— Rabbi Tirzah Firestone, author of *The Receiving: Reclaiming Jewish Women's Wisdom* and *With Roots in Heaven*

Other works
by Jason Shulman

The MAGI Process: A Nondual Method for Personal
Awakening and the Resolution of Conflict

What does reward bring you but to bind you
to Heaven like a slave? (Poetry)

The Instruction Manual for Receiving God

Kabbalistic Healing: A Path to an Awakened Soul

The Master of Hiddenness (Monograph)

Tefillin Psalms (Poetry)

[The Set of the World] (Monograph)

The Work of Briah (Monograph)

Ecstatic Speech

Expressions of True Nonduality

Jason Shulman

THE FOUNDATION
FOR NONDUALITY

The Foundation for Nonduality
Oldwick, New Jersey 08833

Series Editor: Nancy Yielding
Series Managing Editor: Kimberly Burnham
Cover and interior design: Tom Schneider
MS Word *mise-en-scéne:* Jeff Casper

FIRST EDITION 2017

ISBN: 978-0-9972201-1-7

10 9 8 7 6 5 4 3 2 1

Dedication

To the poets and preachers, the brothers and sisters, who heard that silent sound that changes everything. To Li Bo and Tu Fu who fished for poems in mirrors and the Old Master who found the dark and empty ground of all beings in the Valley Spirit. To Jalāl ad-Dīn Muhammad Rūmi and Thomas Treherne, one in the moment and the other in the centuries. To William Blake engraving ecstasy in London and Wallace Stevens selling insurance to heaven in Connecticut and Gerard Hopkins struggling with his song in Dublin. To Homer, who asked stones to tell stories that would last longer than stones, and Christopher Alexander, who uses earthly materials to bring shelter to our souls. And finally, to Walt Whitman, who found his identity in everything and gave every impulse a home in his heart. To everyone, known and unknown, who learned by study or accident or atonement to listen to angels, and tried to say things that could awaken the sleeping pulse of enlightening moments in all of us, this book is dedicated. I bow a grateful bow.

Contents

Preface

Enlightenment seems to be difficult to find mainly because it goes unnoticed by the soul conditioned to ignore the obvious essentials in life. The essentials are these: That the sun rises and sets; that we are born and breathe and live and die; that when we are wounded the world grows smaller and when we are healed we are healed by love. When we are healed by love the world grows larger and there is room for every thing where previously there seemed to be none.

We are also thwarted because we make more of spiritual attainment than we should. Someplace inside of us, we believe enlightenment will set us free from our suffering. Sometimes we have come across misleading or incomplete spiritual tales and writings that underscore this romantic notion. But what awakening actually does is to open a door to our suffering, while simultaneously redeeming it in a new idea of what freedom actually is. We also sometimes believe it will give us new powers and insights: things or thoughts or feelings we have never had before. But what it actually does is make the full spectrum of our birthright—all the things we have *always* had but either did not believe in, see as important, or even have access to—available to us. We remain essentially the same, but different.

The only surprise in awakening is that it was there all along. When we see that, things begin to unroll. We begin to believe that we can feel deeply and wonderfully; we begin to understand the fact that the world is imperfect and perfect at the same time and that when we hold the imperfect world close to our imperfect heart—the world and ourselves being the same thing—laughter and tears are brought together as well. We and the world are made to be a single thing. Finally, we are free. But this freedom is not a freedom *from*, but rather a freedom *with.*

What we call "life" is the union of the faraway and the near. The faraway is the seemingly outer world. The near is ourselves. A nameless, characterless quality pervades and supports both. When this quality is concentrated and localized, we get people and things and worlds. When it is allowed to express its vast nature, we get boundlessness. When both are brought together, we get a *boundless continuity.* "Boundless continuity" might also be called a "bound infinity," that combination of the mortal and the time-bound with the timeless. That is us. And that is actually the best description of what it means to be alive. As people who are in the process of awakening, we have the opportunity to experience the true connection between the faraway and the near. This lets our small and imperfect lives enjoy and depend upon the fruits of eternity.

The texts in *Ecstatic Speech* are all teaching pieces that arise from the place where the particular—that is individuals with pain and sorrow, laughter and joy—and the Silent Eternal meet. They are utterances that give shape to the Absolute and allow this vastness to enter the small chambers of our infinite hearts. In this way we learn our place in the Great Place, a place we sometimes lose because we don't know how to hold our personal suffering along with the Great Perfection we sense within and without our selves. The pieces in this book exist to help us learn that our suffering and our awakening are a single thing, that our imperfections and the Great Perfection arise at exactly the same time and have the same aim, which is freedom.

These pieces are not meant to continue the spiritual exercise of giving us peak experiences of unification, which simply lift us up only to set us down later. The view from the mountaintop is wonderful but so is living in the valley where our towns and neighborhoods are. These pieces extol both views since it is only by union that union is achieved. Said in other words: this is not a book of information but a book of practice.

We achieve the unification of both views—that of the mountaintop and of the valley, of the Absolute and the Relative, and thereby enter the awakening process—by practice. These pieces are meant to be used, sentence by sentence, paragraph by paragraph, by our body, mind and spirit. They are not meant to simply give another psychological or spiritual viewpoint or to add to the conditioned responses we have to the world. They are meant to disarm us so that, arms open, we can embrace who we truly are. We might say that *we* are meant to be used by *them*; that to use these words rightly we are meant to throw ourselves into the practice of taking each word seriously, working through whatever each sentence brings us and seeing *that* as the on-going content of *enlightening* itself. By using them in that way, they become both a living map and a moving vehicle that can take us home.

Some of these pieces are meant to inspire, others to challenge. Some are meant to explain and others to mystify, because real mystification does not obscure, but brings us to things we cannot learn in any other way except by having our conditioned responses to life and learning stopped in their tracks: surrender, love, exquisite quiet and joy that has no reason for being except that it is. Above all, these pieces are meant to bring us into a deepening relationship with all that is, so that our already established partnership, our *prior* engagement with the world—before we were confused and which is our awakening itself—becomes not only visible, but workable, something we can depend upon moment by moment in our daily lives. Enlightenment is not a theoretical position: it is meant to be dinner table conversation and the manners of everyday life.

Enough said. Expect it all. Please go forward.

Jason Shulman
26 December 2016
Truro, Massachusetts

Some Words About Ecstatic Speech

As a writer and teacher, I often find myself at my computer working to put the ideas and thoughts I have about human suffering and the spiritual journey into words. We might say that these hours at the computer are like the farmer's first hours in the field: planning, removing stones and stumps, plowing, planting and waiting. This type of writing, to use another metaphor, is like chipping away at stone. The vision of the final product must be kept in the mind's vision, but the way there is incremental.

Then there is another type of writing that seems to come of its own accord. But, like harvest, it really comes from all the work that went before, work that is now forgotten as the eye catches sight of the first red apple, as the nose lifts itself to the fragrance that heralds Spring.

The pieces in this collection are of the second type. I experience their creation as a force within my body, a combination of a rhythm and a voice, a sort of whispering I open my body to, which then becomes an actual utterance, the hard work momentarily lost as I enter as into the delight of expression.

At the same time, these pieces, when they come, are not about some sort of spontaneous speech whose main objective is the delivery of some emotion or feeling, heightened or rarefied. What I mean by *ecstatic speech* is not speech or writing about a feeling of happiness, spiritual or otherwise. It is not about whirling emotions or of being temporarily lifted to a new plane of consciousness. Instead, it is speech that revels in precision and clarity as well as poetry; it allows the reader to participate in the openness from which the original words sprang, lifting *them* from one world of being to another.

Another thing that true ecstatic speech should do is to include the totality of what it means to be human, with all of its glory and possibility and all of its suffering and imperfection. In this way we find a home in the project of enlightenment, which is to say, find an awakening to our True Nature.

By its very nature, ecstatic speech has no sense of propriety. It is direct, blunt, and not a slave to convention. It can be rude or anything else it needs to be to further human freedom. And such speech, in its written form, can be read and used on many levels. After years of study and even as the author of these pieces, I still find inspiration and education in them. The work never stops—another thing that ecstatic speech teaches us. As the *Flower Ornament Sutra,* (also known as the *Avatamsaka Sutra,* one of the foundational texts of Kegon Buddhism) teaches us, "Buddhas are beings who are greatly enlightened about their delusions; ordinary beings are those who are greatly deluded by their enlightenment." And onward we go in our imperfect way, falling in and out of awakening and nonduality.

The "project of enlightenment" I mentioned above is always about the human ego and the problems inherent in believing that the ego's point of view is the only one and not simply a particular syntax. The moment of creation of all ecstatic speech is that point in time where the signaling of this truth manages to get through and tell us this *vérité:* that the ego has a home in enlightenment; that once integrated on a deep level, this separateness that causes so many of our problems is what beauty is made of.

My motive in writing these pieces has always been to bring people—if they follow the texts carefully—an *experience* of awakening rather than just a description. This is an unorthodox methodology that brings the seeker to the territory itself; it does not simply portray the map or list what we will find there. Ecstatic speech does not continue to split the world but shows a new version of what Wholeness is, one in which the suffering of our split self can be included in Wholeness, which, in fact, *must* be included in Wholeness in order for us to be free. This is what these "ecstatic teaching texts" can help us with. Simple, even poetic descriptions of ecstasy are not the only conduit to enlightenment. In diving into our suffering in just the right way we can also arrive at the truth about Reality. These pieces can be studied, each sentence held in the body, mind and spirit until it ripens to reveal its nectar and most importantly, its power to heal and help.

I hope you find stories or paragraphs, sentences, words or syllables that free you. Perhaps you will find a single vowel that will fill you with light. That would certainly be enough.

Thoughts About True Nonduality

In the mid-1960's, when I began to formalize my spiritual quest, I had an experience one day, sitting in my near-to-the college apartment on Ditmas Avenue in Brooklyn. I had somehow come upon the *Gospel of Sri Ramakrishna* and was reading one day, taking a break from my duties as editor-in-chief of the college literary magazine. I don't remember the passage I read, but my head exploded. It was just like that: a sense of infinite light and the understanding of a simple thing: *all things were only and totally themselves.*

Looking back over my journals and writing from those years recently, I saw that the spiritual themes I was dealing with then were the same themes I had dealt with for years: the seeming conflict between the theistic God-centered approaches of Western religions and the nondual, advaitic, non-theistic approach mostly identified with the East, the first seemingly *personal*, the other, seemingly transcendent and impersonal.

I found my spiritual path bounced backed and forth between various poles. Sometimes I felt the need to surrender my self to a "higher power," to a creator spirit, a personal God. I felt the need to pray, to sing to the Divine Spirit, to ask Heaven for help, to lower my expectations that I could do anything myself.

Other times, wanting to be free from what then appeared to be a split between me and the universe, I simply sat *zazen*–Zen meditation–and began to realize the great spaciousness and nonduality of the "mind-only" approach, something I thought could achieve by my own efforts. Anything else seemed superfluous. Then, that approach would grow cold and my suffering as a human being–along with its inherent humility– would arise again, and off I would go, seeking God and God's help.

Sometimes I bemoaned the fact that I wasn't a "steady" practitioner; that I moved from side to side in this internal and intense drama. I did not do this frivolously, but still I allowed my approach to change as I needed it to change. At some point, I began to realize, to slowly understand, that I was being given a tour of the various approaches to spiritual awakening and that I was trying to explore a deep and prior understanding in myself that would not be moved, namely, that all of these approaches were not only *not* irreconcilable, but that *they must be a single thing on some level of understanding.* In other words, they must be simply different views of the same thing.

What I began to understand and put into practice in my life and teaching, was that what we call the "self" is really a continuum of syntaxes, a spectrum of intensities, from completely separate on one hand, to completely united with the cosmos on the other. And further, that this "self," as a notion of intensities and colorations, was not a "thing" in and of itself. And further, that it could be valid and authentic at any given point along its continuum. Said in different words, any specific version of the "the self" can be limited and neurotic or whole and free; our ability to make this choice depends upon our awakening to the fact that, while none of these positions are our true identity, they can be our true experience and expression of our Real Self.

Seeing the truth of the relationship between the Relative and Absolute, we become healed and stronger, more vivid and alive. As we allow ourselves to have a broader and wider view of *what is*, our own *who-is* begins to relate not to the momentarily fixed version of the self, but to something more powerful, more universal, more loving and more constant—even as we honor and devote ourselves to our chosen way.

Which brings me back to Ramakrishna. Ramakrishna was a devotee of the Mother. The strange and unique thing about him was that he knew many, many parts of this spectrum of the self, from totally separate to completely united. He "descended" in a sense, from the totally nondual position to continuing to be what he always really was, a child of the Mother. But his deep understanding and embodiment of nonduality filtered all he was through the quartz of the nondual view. This has turned out to be my personal path.

An example: in Pure Land Buddhism, we chant to *Amida Buddha*. From this perspective, Amida is a separate entity or condition of universal consciousness. But if we continue with our chanting and spiritual work, we discover, amazingly enough, that *we are Amida*. We are Amida in the sense that beneath all of our personality quirks, we are the embodiment of a "calling," which is the force that actually drives our life, whether we are conscious of it or not. And this calling *is Amida himself.* Separate and not separate. One and also two. This is true nonduality. Are you seeking God or is God seeking you? Why do you have these thoughts of liberation? Who put them there? These are not philosophical or intellectual questions: they are at the basis of all our lives.

In *Ecstatic Speech* you will find poems to God, hymns to the Mother and dialogues with Amida Buddha, along with the pure sound of nondual Silence and the bright light of the *Thusness* of all of creation. You will also find commentary that suggests ways to practically work with these texts to reclaim the Wholeness that is already there.

From my feeling, one of our greatest gifts is that we can have all of these perspectives since we need all the help we can get! And all the help we need is available and the totality of all views are available *in each one of these views.* The universe, it turns out, is totally holographic and fractal, each view a microcosm of the whole, a recapitulation designed to enlighten us. All of these gods are one. All of these words exist only to set us free.

Why I Sometimes Number My Paragraphs

1. Because I see each sentence as a proposition and not prose; something to be worked at, worked on, and worked through and with. With prose, our mind goes into a conventional mode, skimming parts, grouping words together so that we can get the sense quickly and easily. We miss the sound. And, as the great Jewish prayer of the Shema tells us, the realization of God's Singleness (read here: the unifying Wholeness of Reality...) starts with the word *Shema*, which means "Listen!" Here, I want the reader to linger over each paragraph and find its power. To hear its Voice. I first saw this methodology used by the Viennese philosopher Ludwig Wittgenstein. Of course, he learned it from someone else and we're still trying to find the fellow that started the whole thing...

Introduction:
This Song, This Life

There is a deep notion in every spiritual seeker, often hidden in the best of intentions, a belief that awakening or enlightenment will clear away the complexities of the relative or dualistic world and present us with utter clarity, something we can be sure of, something not infiltrated by our own prejudices. We hope enlightenment will not be a relative thing but something rock steady and diamond bright.

But the truth is: everything is a syntax. Because everything is truly connected, everything is in mutually co-arising relationship. Because of this, everything is not only dependent upon everything else, but affects the life of everything else. If we look at the world through a red filter, everything will take on a red hue. When we look at ourselves and the world, everything is psychosomatic, in the original root meaning of the word: everything is *body/mind.* So we sit with our body/mind, we speak with our body/mind and so on. There is no mind/body dualism: they are different expressions of the same thing. Not only that: the way we are built and the perceptual apparatus we already have puts a *prior* editorial prejudice on everything we encounter in the inner and outer world. The world is filled with lifting and touching because we have hands. The world is filled

1

with delusion and truth because we have a mind that tends to perceive the world in those terms. We build the metaphors and philosophies of our world based solely on our own experience: The world *is* the context of our own mechanism. We and the world are intertwined. We can never leave it for some other realm.

This may be a disappointment to some who are still hoping to find a way of clarity *through* all of this relative contextualization. But it is actually cause for hope. The understanding that *everything is syntax* is ultimately freeing. It allows us to let go of "our" truth, "our" understanding by the act of *including* it *knowingly,* in an awakened manner. It takes the *personal* itself, and helps us understand that the personal is simply and only a syntax—never-ending—as long as we are "a person." Seeing this clearly is to let go of it a bit. Then and only then, can we begin to appreciate that there are other syntaxes, that sometimes there are many contexts going on at the same time and that awakening is—as it always was—about seeing what is actually going on and not about seeing some fantastical ultimate truth. We might say that the ultimate truth is that there is no ultimate truth *except* this entire system taken as it is.

The great Zen master Dogen-zenji said *the mountains and rivers are walking.* In what syntax does this take place? In what syntax is the whole world so alive that everything pulsates and lives in the bubbling moment?

This first piece is an expression of this truth. It is about the unity of the relative and absolute and how they interact. In fact, it is not "about" anything. It is the simple utterance that arises of its own accord through us as beings, from the very fact of Oneness.

This is the story of an inter-dependent world.

This Song, This Life

1. You cannot see the Real.

2. All we can see is the UnReal before we see it as the Real.

3. The Unreal is anything that is separate or seen as separate from the Real.

4. An example: We see the apple without the tree; we see the lake without the underground stream that feeds it. We see the tree without the roots.

5. We are constantly and forever in a context, a syntax. This is what separateness is or seems to be.

6. We can only see the syntax (if we put our mind to it).

7. Once we see the impossibility of ever getting free of syntax, of stages, of particles, of pieces, what then?

8. Then, the Thing we cannot look at appears and we are wrapped in it. *Rapt* by it.

9. We are then completely free. Free to be in the context of our choosing and the context we *do not choose.*

10. And what of this invisible Thing? *It holds the world together.*

11. And what is the world? *What we make of it.*

12. Compassion comes from seeing the web we have made by our eyes. Our eyes and ears. Our bodies and mind.

13. We realize our thoughts—every one of them— are syntax, are contexts.

14. I need to repeat this: We realize our thoughts— every one of them—are syntax, are contexts.

15. And then we are free once more to *not look.*

16. When we *do not look at the invisible but are aware of it, are of the same family as it,* we See.

17. In Seeing, we See an empty room.

18. This empty room is one we can live in. We can move the furniture around, we can *take our eyes off life*, that is, no longer look too closely, with tension and effort, *because we are Loved.*

19. Who are we loved by? That which we cannot see, but which *rapts* us, enwraps us.

20. Then all of our thoughts become ladders and our hearts become ladders and we can move these ladders to any treetop, to any roof, climb up and look.

21. We see our human life then. All of our culture, which is all syntax. We are not caught by light or Light; not enmeshed or categorized.

22. We fold into our human destiny, our wrinkled skin, the one we came out with and the one we go into.

23. But we peer at all this with bright eyes.

24. We look, playing with memory as a context, but never really believing it is the Real; knowing it is the Real's Companion.

25. Help is on the Road. The Road itself is Help.

26. It turns out that everything is Help. Help for nothing: there is nothing to Help. Or we only help until we come to understand that Help is the Activity we were born for. It is the Activity of the Road.

27. We could break down now and simply call it Love, but this is Love we cannot see, whether in the early morning or the late afternoon. We walk through it like air. It is our Life.

28. Now it is about to rain. Or not. Let's watch it drop like something from Heaven. Like something we were born to watch. Like something we are made of.

Introduction:
Dialogues with Amitabha

I came upon Amitabha through the kind help of Roshi Kendo Rich Hart. Speaking to him one evening, I said *I'm tired of learning through suffering. I want to learn through joy.* He suggested a book called *Embracing Despair, Discovering Peace.* It seemed like a good place to start.

Since then, the Pure Land school of Buddhism has become one of my joys. It mirrored most exactly my own prior belief, that we are imperfect beings who cannot prosper and be free as long as we believe we are completely separate and autonomous beings. Pure Land Buddhism is not about gain so much as about loss: the loss of blaming ourselves for not being perfect; the loss of the belief that by gaining some sort of knowledge or understanding we will become powerful in some way that allows us to rise above our troubles. Pure Land is based on this fact: that we are foolish beings who can *never, never, never* stop being foolish, which is to say, resistant, selfish, short-sighted and ego-centric. Pure Land believes that once we have asserted the truth of this, when we are no longer resisting what is an obvious fact, Amida Buddha enters our lives and we are "reborn" in the Pure Land, which is the liberated version of the here and now. When I say "liberated," I mean it's exactly the same as it was *before* it was liberated, but with the addition of the infinite kindness of this Buddha, who cares for and looks out for each one of us. Does this seem foolish in and of itself? A fantasy? A child's dream? You must try it yourself before you can decide.

For me, it is one of the most sophisticated approaches to the task of being Real. Amida Buddha—the Japanese name for *Amitabha,* the Buddha of Infinite Life and Light, was originally, as the mythopoetic story goes, a monk named Dharmakara. He said to Lord Buddha one day, *What good is it to become a Buddha? If I become a Buddha, and someone cannot—by calling on me even one time!—be born into the Pure Land, then what good is it?*

Now Dharmakara *became* a Buddha and by doing so, the Vow—one of eighteen great vows he made—was fulfilled. It was fulfilled because through his completed vow, the unalterable pathway between *call* and *response* was made. In this way, our sincere *calling* is our enlightenment. This is nonduality at its most deep: when *two* become *one* and remain *separate.* Pure Land adherents *call upon the Name of Amida* by saying or chanting: *Namu Amida Butsu,* which is to say, "I take refuge in Amida Buddha." This "taking refuge" is no small thing: it comes from the certainty that you can never be certain, that you can never be finished, that your imperfection is intricately braided into who you are and can never be conquered. But that by seeing and knowing that truth, we are liberated. Amida in us is liberated into our consciousness. Who we truly are, arrives.

These dialogues encompass some of my instantaneous understanding of who I and Amida are. They arrive for all of us in that moment when time disappears and is replaced by Great Faith.

Dialogues with Amitabha

Dialogue 1

Me: Dear Amitabha: Who am I?

Amitabha: You are the part that sings.

Me: I sing?

Amitabha: Yes. You sing to me.

Me: What do I sing? What song? How do I know the words?

Amitabha: You sing me your suffering.

Me: I do?

Amitabha: Yes. To find your suffering clearly enough is to locate me among the stars, is to find the Buddha-field I created and live in. It is to locate yourself.

Me: Then it's an achievement!

Amitabha: Yes it is.

Me: Of course, I shouldn't say that: that is only strengthening my ego, my self-power, and I should be relinquishing it.

Amitabha: You and I can dispense with self-power and other-power: we are friends. My Name, who I am, extends through three worlds. I claim your errant self-power as my own. You don't have to worry about it.

Me: So there is a change and there is no change.

Amitabha: What do you mean?

Me: My self-power remains, my confusions, my suffering. And yet, when it is part of you, I no longer take it as my own.

Amitabha: This is true. Should I call you grasshopper now?

Me: Yes, that would be good! To have a father-teacher!

Amitabha: I will be your father-teacher and your mother-teacher.

Me: When I think of you this way, you are quite large...

Amitabha: I am. I fill the heavens and I fill the earth. When someone wakes up, what they recognize is their own suffering. They do not wake up to Me. They arise within their own consciousness as the one who is suffering. They see themselves as the suffering being and not one who is being suffered upon. Then, seeing this mite of a world for what it is, I come treading.

Me: You come treading...?

Amitabha: I come treading, world-walking, world-spanning, molecule and atom standing, and I reveal myself.

Me: You reveal yourself?

Amitabha: Yes, I reveal Myself to be the World. In this way, each thing becomes a bodhisattva not because it has changed its nature in any way, but because it has *found* its nature.

Me: And what is its nature?

Amitabha: That each thing is entirely useful. That each thing is entirely itself and nothing but itself. That each thing exists only in a vast web that doesn't hold the world together because it *is* the world.

Me: Then that's why I feel at home, truly settled when I see you, when I hear you, when I feel you in the air, curving because you are the Curver of All Things.

Amitabha: Yes. My Nature is the Arc that is truly Intimate, the Most Contactful, Never Leaving you Alone!

Me: I feel at home...

Amitabha: You feel at home because home appears when you awaken to what actually is.

Me: ...and that is?

Amitabha: Stop this pretense!

Me: What actually is, is sunrise and sunset. What actually is, is the curve of singular love, so minute and so grand that every insect loves its home, that every child knows its mother, that the world is constant food and blessing.

Amitabha: This you know. Now my Name and your name are a singular event, a Certain Sun. One Word. You take Refuge in the Sheltering Air.

Me: I take Refuge in the Sheltering Air.

Amitabha: And in this way, we become One.

Dialogue 2

Me: I want to become one with you. That is the heart of my effort. Sometimes I feel at-one-ment with you, but then it disappears.

Amitabha: You can never be one with me.

Me: You don't understand: As an incomplete being, a being who will forever be incomplete, I search for you as you search for me. In you I find my completion, my wholeness, the end of my search.

Amitabha: You can never complete yourself in Me.

Me: What are you saying? This is devastating!

Amitabha: You can never complete yourself in me because you are *un-complete-able*. You seek to complete yourself so that you do not have to face this basic truth: you are partial. You are not of my realm. You cannot create the Pure Land. You cannot transform. You cannot change.

Me: But isn't the whole point *to change?* Isn't the whole point to grow, to fathom the mystery of your existence, of wholeness, of the Complete?

Amitabha: No. The whole point is for you to see who you are and for me to see who I am.

Me: And never the twain shall meet?

Amitabha: I didn't say that. In fact, that question is irrelevant. Even more: that question is an obstacle to your main purpose: *to simply see who you are.*

Me: To see my smallness? My ineptitude? My inability, after a lifetime of practice, to have made much progress? And by that, I don't mean progress as the world sees it. I mean progress as my heart knows it...

Amitabha: Yes. That is your job. I have my job and you have your job.

Me: But that is...unbearable on some level.

Amitabha: How do you know?

Me: I suppose that this is true.

Amitabha: Your supposition is just that: fantasy. Consider for a moment that all of your life you have been carrying a burden: that you are *something,* that you are important. What an extra weight! A water-wheel turns because it is designed in a certain way and placed in a stream of moving water. It does not think of itself as *important*. Any such thought would be *extra*, and would actually interfere with its function. Another example: you love your grandson. You have two choices in this love: the first is to be constantly surprised by feeling so much love for something so small, a being that does so little but one who, when he does anything at all, lights up the universe. The second way is: *Oh! I love my grandson. Isn't that wonderful! It feels so good to love! I wonder if he loves me too....* And on and on.

What a burden it is to live a lie, to carry around *beliefs* instead of facts. Facts are simple: you are you. You have good intentions. You carry them out very imperfectly. You are greedy, selfish, arrogant, and so on. These are not sins! It is no more a sin than saying *I am a pine tree* (when you are that...), or: *I am a stream of rushing water* (when you are that...).

You are looking for your true nature, your *subjective nature*, the only nature you can truly know. When you see that true nature a kind of joy breaks forth, a lightness of spirit. Gravity fails to pull you down to hell and instead lets you stand up straight.

That joy, that gravity, that lightness is Who I Am.

Me: And then I can become one with you?

Amitabha: No. When you see your own nature, if you are brave enough to see it completely, or, since you are imperfect, when you know that you see it imperfectly (!), *you*, as you are, disappear. You become like a red cardinal flying low to the green ground. You become the food the bird searches for, the wings that air flows around. You don't *become* me. Instead, you begin to see that *I was always there, that I am made of the same material as sorrow but without that name.* You Are. I Am. Which one of us is the red bird?

What you call "you" is the burden you carry. The lie. Lay the lie down and see what you call yourself then.

Me: Amitabha! Amitabha!

Amitabha: Yes?

Me: I'm just trying out this new Name, the Name everything answers to when I have laid my burdens down.

Amitabha: Jason!

Me: Yes?

Amitabha: You are a good man.

Dialogue 3

Me: I have discovered the power of being myself.

Amitabha: Tell me about it.

Me: Lying in bed one night with my wife, she picked up a book and read me a passage. I don't remember the details but it basically said *bind yourself to your karma.*

Amitabha: I wrote that...

Me: No, it was someone else, someone Japanese...

Amitabha: No, you misunderstand *Me: I* wrote that!

Me: Oh, you mean...well, anyway, I've been trying that. I find it is better than trying to purify my imperfect self away, educate it away or even surrender it away. *I bind myself to it. I stay awake as I dock with it, like a spaceship docking with a space station. I get connected.* And then, something happens.

Amitabha: What is that, pray tell?

Me: Instead of feeling trapped, I feel free: this is *just me*. And in being *just me*, I see that it is both me and not-me at the same time.

Amitabha: Can you explain that?

Me: Yes: *its just who I am* on one hand and when I connect to it in this way, it *collapses* into something very small. It no longer fills the air with danger or its furtive song. It becomes like a rock in a stream: the rock doesn't control the stream. It modifies that portion of it, but basically, the water flows on. The air is clear.

Amitabha: You are mixing metaphors!

Me: I can't help myself.

Amitabha: Neither can I!

Me: So, I become the rock *and* the stream. They were meant to co-exist. There is no problem. I am not controlled by a pebble, no matter how large...

Amitabha: So you wrote that!

Me: No no no! I don't want to take credit for that! Its *you* in one of your many guises...

Amitabha: Not good enough.

Me: What do you mean?

Amitabha: You are still afraid of your own power.

Me: My power corrupts me. It leads me astray.

Amitabha: So being led astray is not me? I have a border, an ending-place?

Me: Well...that doesn't seem logical does it...

Amitabha: Allow me to become large. I do not belong to you.

Me: How large?

Amitabha: Dear Heart: Allow me to become large until the world grows fuzzy and is filled with lightening sparks, inside and outside a single display.

Me: ...of what?

Amitabha: My Face. Your power, my power: who are we to divide the world in this way? It is simply a matter of ownership: You don't own this power...and neither do I.

Me: Then...?

Amitabha: Then Nothing. What is there to say? Do you think there is nothing I am in awe of? When I am alone, I might believe that. But when I am with you, then I am in awe. You might say I *am* awe itself. There is nothing left of me.

Me: I am afraid.

Amitabha: That's ok. Go sit in a chair. Think about the night, the slowly darkening sky. Blue to dark blue to black. Feel the trees give off oxygen as the sun descends. Breathe it in. Make your vowels long enough to express pleasure.

Me: This is...difficult.

Amitabha: I'd be a fool to deny it. Beside that, I cannot speak. I am the One Without Words. I leave my speaking to you.

Dialogue 4

Me: I am knocking at your door.

Amitabha: Come in!

Me: I am knocking at your door!

Amitabha: Come in, come in!

Me: Wow! The last thing I remember was thinking, *I'd like to be with Amitabha.* Now, suddenly it seems to me, I'm in here with you, sitting by the fire...

Amitabha: Yes, it seemed sudden to me too! Why don't...

Me: I'm knocking at your door!

Amitabha (opening the door): You know, you were just in here, we were talking together, enjoying the fire and suddenly you disappeared....

Me: I don't remember. I remember knocking...

Amitabha: Come in...again. Sit down. Let me examine you. OK. You seem to be in good health but I keep sensing that there is something missing. What could it be? How's your memory?

Me: Perfect!

Amitabha: OK. What's my name?

Me: Amida.

Amitabha: Nope. That's not it. And I don't mean "Amitabha;" that's just one of my names. But: what's my name?

Me: It's not Amitabha?

Amitabha: No. My name is Namu Amida Butsu.

Me: Ah, I see.

Amitabha: What do you see?

Me: I see the self and the Self as One. The seeker and the seen as One. The one who bows and waits is waiting for the one who bows and waits.

Amitabha: Are you thirsty? I sense we'd both love a cup of tea...

Introduction:
In the Clutches of the Great Bear Mother

Impersonal Movement® is a form of moving meditation developed that focuses on setting up the conditions to experience the Unitive State. It is a spiritual tool designed to bring its practitioners to an experience of their own fundamental nature.

The practice of IM allows us to directly experience the change of perspective we have heard spiritual masters speak of—to pass through the doorway of personal attachment and enter the endless Place of our origin. Whether we call it " letting go of the ego," "transcendence," "God-consciousness," "Enlightenment," "Wholeness or Awakening," it is this we come into relationship with in the practice of IM.

This piece has been used by my advanced students as a kind of roadmap. However—and this is important to note—*you don't have to be a student of this particular discipline to have experienced what it is like to walk into the unknown with all the best of intentions, hoping to gain more clarity and insight into yourself and your place in the universe and encountering what we might—in the psychological age, call "resistance."*

To counter our resistance, there resides in the universe—who knows where!—an opposite force that demands, calls forth and

25

insists upon awakening. This force resides in each of us, in that part that is not only personal. In this piece this calling appears as the Great Bear Mother.

Every one of us who has attempted to walk the road of the spirit has had many encounters with the Great Bear Mother, that implacable life-force that simply cannot take "no" for an answer. All difficult moments in our lives, whether they are with partners and mates, with illness or health, with friends or foes, are actually encounters with the Great Bear. It is important for spiritual seekers to reframe their so-called resistance in this way, since even their resistance to spiritual achievement is not entirely personally-owned! (More about that later.) But it is important to remember that much of what we take for our recalcitrance is actually our ignorance as to what this vivid force is and assuming it is just another incarnation of our personal neurosis.

Some of my advanced students have kept a diary of their encounters, day by day with the Great Bear Mother. If you do this too, you will come to realize just how much contact you have with the universal spirit personified in this form. Knowing that, your journey will grow easier and your destination closer.

Note: As I mentioned elsewhere, the paragraphs are numbered so that each one stands by itself as a unit to think about and as a thing to do, to put into action. You can spend years working with this song of enlightenment.

In the Clutches of the Great Bear Mother

1. To be in the clutches of the Great Bear Mother is to be involved in a completely non-egoic event.

2. Walking into the cave, it is at first only darkness. You hear stirrings in the back of the cave but you cannot see them. You walked into the cave of your own free will but now you wonder why you ended up at this destination at all. It seems ridiculous. You know you are looking for trouble.

3. What happens next cannot be described. It cannot be described not because it is so mystical or deeply hidden or anything like that, but because *we never know what will take place and what our reaction will be.* Entering the cave we have left behind the logic of small things: action and reaction.

4. One of the first things we realize as we take our journey into the cave of the Great Bear Mother is that this cave has no specific location: It is not in the mountains or in the valley, in the country or in the city. In fact, it is a moveable cave and shows up where and when it wants to. In other words, even here, we are not in charge of the Great Bear Mother, or what she decides to do or when she decides to do it.

5. For instance: You want to go to the movies and the line is too long and you are left without tickets. If you are feeling ok about this, the Great Bear Mother is there, but her claws are sheathed and she remains in the back of the cave, silent, contemplating the eternal.

6. If you are upset to the extent that something in you feels destroyed or injured, that injury itself is the stirring of the Great Bear Mother, coming into what we might call a state of arousal, rising like a giant wave. You smell her there, moist and wet. She lumbers toward you ready to point this injury out to you and to ask you a great question: *Can you remain awake and feel this injury? Do you need to leave and take a holiday from reality? Or can you step further into the cave, back toward the force that you have spent your life avoiding?*

7.   These seem like small questions: Movies?
     Tickets? Really we are talking about life and
     death. Getting what we want. Losing what we
     have.

8.   We must remember as we talk about this, that
     the Great Bear Mother is also not just some
     sort of natural force without rhyme or reason.
     The Great Bear Mother is not a hurricane or
     earthquake. She is the highest intelligence of
     the Universe. But to commune with her, to
     sport with her, we must learn what she is trying
     to teach us and what she is trying to teach is
     well beyond letting go to the involuntary forces
     of the universe. It is way beyond simply
     walking into the unknown as well.

9.   In the language of the Great Bear Mother,
     speaking is the same as silence; the unknown is
     the same as the known; the cave is everywhere
     there is in the outside world and yet resides in
     the center of the heart.

10. The Great Bear Mother is utterly dependable.
     If you say she is capricious you have not met
     her. If you say she is arbitrary, you have not
     felt her claws. Likewise, if you say she resides
     in one place and that her address can be found,
     you have made your home on a floating island

in the middle of a raging river and you will soon drown.

11. The Great Bear Mother does not demand anything of you except all you have. When you show up completely in any place at all, Mother is there to lift you up, high above her head so that you can get a glimpse of the view. When you show up asleep, carried to her den by the dark currents of what-ever-is, she will ignore you, disguise herself so that you cannot see her black fur against the black night, or hold you under the cold water until you awake.

12. If the Great Bear Mother were simply the "unknown," then we could make a sort of peace with that. We would know where she resided. It would be called "over there," or "the farther shore," or "gone beyond, gone well-beyond." It would not be here.

13. But the Great Bear Mother is neither the known nor the unknown, neither the big nor the small. She is only herself and, when we are ready to know her, she reveals herself as our own deepest self as well.

14. What do you know of yourself? Who are you? What do you think keeps you alive? Why do

the molecules of your skin hang together? Why did your brain form?

15. As we ask these questions, everything that is not us falls away. Our ideas and thoughts, our pet peeves, our inconsistencies, our irrational anger, our timidity, our carelessness, our self-consciousness. Everything.

16. What is left is the Great Bear Mother who has been hiding in our own skin, the streaming force that made the world, that *is* the world. The Mother who watches out for her cubs, who essentially *is* her cubs: same fur, same blood, same tissue, same huge bear thoughts that think up the universe every afternoon.

17. When we put ourselves in the clutches of the Great Bear Mother, bear meets bear in the darkened cave. It is a meeting you are not likely to forget. This strong light melts our bones. We become cellophane, layers of luminosity within light.

18. But being human, we *will* forget it and go back to reading stories about what it is like in the cave, how to feed the bear, be with the bear, negotiate terrain with the bear and how to bring bear presents to the bear so that the bear won't kill us.

19. But there is no *community* in this, no
    communing either. We need the invocation of
    the ancient mantra to awaken again.

20. Here is the prayer of the Great Bear Mother:
    Hello! What will you do with me today? I
    might fight you today. I might go along with
    you on a journey, I might sing to you: Will you
    sing to me? Here, let me lose myself in your
    deep fur. Here, feel my fur! Help, I have no
    fur! Help I don't know anything! Help! Help!
    Help!

21. Sincerely spoken, this prayer will always bring
    out the best in the Great Bear Mother and she
    will respond. We could put this another way
    entirely: Spoken sincerely, this prayer will
    bring out the best in *you*, and you will awaken
    to what the universe is and who you are, and
    you will truly respond when spoken to. You
    will hear what people say. You will not be in a
    trance of your own history or language or
    anything else. You will become a bear in a cave
    and wait for someone to find you, to dare to
    enter your domain while you wait, wet and
    dense near the back wall, willing to wait and
    see what happens.

22. You will reward bravery with bravery. When you meet bravery you will dance and sing and roar. *I am the Great Bear Mother! My dance is beyond movement and stillness because it is both and neither. These are not the rules I live by. Yet I live by just and understandable rules. I am not without pity, though I am without sentimentality. I am not so mysterious that I cannot be talked about, approached, touched, kissed and fucked. I will do those same things to you.*

23. All around us are forces that exist in our everyday lives. They centrifuge us around a sun, and like planets, we create gravity so that there can be life in us.

24. That is all the Great Bear Mother is: *Life.*

25. Do you want life?

26. *Then walk into the cave of your own heart and be with whatever you find there.*

27. Do you want life?

28. *Then walk into your resistance with utter kindness. Not contempt. Hold yourself like a mother holds her cubs. Be awake and touch your own heart.*

29. The Great Bear Mother sings in her cave. Her song is lonely when you are not there because she loves having all of creation with her, infinite multitudes within the confines of her small, rounded home.

30. Her song is glorious because she knows wherever you are, you are with her, that you cannot leave the country that has no borders, the universe that has no end.

31. *She waits for you.*
    You wait for her.
    So go.

Introduction:
The Origin and Destiny of Me

Here is something astounding to think about: Buddhism teaches us that there is no permanent self. People think of this as meaning that the self does not exist. This is not true. And searching for this as truth has been the ruin of many a poor man, as the song goes. You are reading this. To say this is not true is insane. And yet...

At the same time, this self *only exists in the present moment.* Part of the problem is that this existing-present-moment-self likes to project itself back into the past and forward into the future, as if it had actual *duration!* It does not. It exists, but in a limited way.

When we start seeing the validity of the self-in-the-present-moment, and treat its belief in its existence-over-time with the true kindness we reserve for small children, we will begin to get somewhere.

The Origin and Destiny of Me

1.   The sentences of me come together in the
     moment the way sunlight (at that moment)
     bends our vision (at that moment) toward the
     edge of leaves, coronal illumination, sun and
     eye. At that moment there is me.

2.   The sentences of me come together and make
     me, not *me* having been present in the past or
     me who will be present in the future.

3.   The present me can think of these things and
     does, trying to get a fix on what it is. It doesn't
     know but thinks it must be some *thing* since
     everything it sees seems to be some *thing* too.

4.   So it carries its past as a present thing and
     thinks of its future as a present thing. It makes
     a house. Lives there, streaming.

5. One stream of water (why is it flowing?) hits
another, one cold, the other warm, much
warmer. A fog appears over the water where
the two streams touch. Neither stream is foggy
but fogginess appears where the streams kiss.
That is me there, hovering above the waters
that gave me birth but have nothing to do with
me. In the next moment, some wind blows the
fog away. The streams mix and warm the coast
of England, out from the Gulf right here.

6. The sentences of me fill the gulf that is not
there. Fill it with something, something real
and not real, there and not there.

7. Me is present only in the present.

8. Because me is afraid and temporary and
silently always knows this, it surrounds itself
with time like a fat suit, like flesh, like a parka
in time, brings forward past and future so
called, and pretends it takes up space.

9. But now: you. And now: you again. No thing in
the stream of the world called you. But you
appear even now, considering and fearful.

10. If we watch these sentences come together, we
are not of this book only. Then joy for eyes and
I; then happiness for a point of view; then

remarkable memories of ice flows, collisions,
intimate relationships on board a vast steamer,
steaming into unknown seas.

Introduction:
The Silent Body

From a dualistic point of view, the Great Mother, or Shakti, exists as a being in some realm with which we have interaction. From the point of view of nonduality, words and terms like the "Great Mother" and "Shakti" *are us.* Dualistically, we can say that "gold is of a yellow color..." as if "gold" and its "yellow color" were two different things. But they are not. Our life and our breathing, though it is often useful to think of them as separate items (as for example, when we need to think about pathological illnesses in the lungs), they are one and the same. The air never ends for a bird; the sea is endless for a fish. Since both "fish" and "bird" cease to exist as such when there is no air or water, fish and water, air and bird are a unified whole. In the same way, we are one with the world.

The Silent Body is a teaching text meant to be studied and used. It takes the reader—the user, really—step by step through different levels of consciousness and describes the movement in consciousness from the symbolic body to the naturally silent and illuminated body. The naturally illuminated body is not something we gain, but it is something we lose. We lose it not by death but by paying attention only to the separate-only consciousness and making believe it is the *totality of our being.*

We only see what our separateness really is—a sort of glory!—when we have ceased insisting that the smallest part of ourselves (our un-integrated egos) is really the largest part of ourselves. When the ego is healed and cherished, the Silent Body appears. When we find out how to enter the Silent Body, the ego integrates into the whole more deeply and we See.

This is a Prajnaparamita text. Prajnaparamita means "the perfection of transcendent wisdom." It is often personified as a female deity, Astasahasrika. And though transcendent wisdom is beyond gender, it is always a good thing to return to your Mother

The Silent Body

1. The silent body is without thought, beneath story and beyond conceptualization. Because it is these things, it is in the province of the Great Mother, Shakti.

2. The Great Mother Shakti, who is not a person, who is not an object, who is not separate from us in anyway, can only appear when the body is no longer a ghost.

3. The body is a ghost when it narrates life to feel alive instead of living it.

4. To achieve the silent body, the body must return to truth and leave—at least for a while—symbolic speech.

5. Symbolic speech arises when the bodymind—which is limited in time to Now—tries to experience a Now as if this now could be somewhere, somewhen else than

where it is now, someplace pristine that does not include its totality.

6. Symbolic speech arises when we listen to the echo instead of to the sound.

7. Symbolic speech arises when the mind—which is the thinking part of the body—makes the body its psychological shadow and tells the story it believes is true instead of the one that is actual.

8. It then enters "story" and is in the realm of the representational, the symbol for the thing instead of the thing.

9. On the road to the silent body, we must encounter the body-as-corpse, the body that is all in history, since the true Now has not been found or experienced.

10. Seeing that the body is in history is part of seeing the body in the actual Now.

11. We fear letting the body return to the silence of non-symbolic speech, the speech of no sound, no place but here, no strategy but our actions in the moment. Our mind believes that aliveness must be made in its own image. The fear is that, allowing the body to return to

silence, we will lose who we are. In other words, thinking we are the body in some narrow image of now, some idea of the now, any change threatens our existence, any relaxing brings us the fear that we will disappear.

12. Our mind in its present state has a small identity. We have an innate psychic part of our minds that fears any change, whether for good or ill, which believes it needs to make the world over in its own image, within its own imagination, in order to survive.

13. When the world changes—for change it must— this unhealed ego, this troublesome part that will eventually become our friend—fears for its life.

14. So, as infant and child, young adult, adult and elder, if we are unknown to ourselves, we work to keep life small and, though professing the love of growth and change, work for its enemies instead.

15. Thus the movement into the *first* stage of oneness—when we experience the pure unity of all things without the later addition of *difference*—is difficult.

16. This first experience is the experience in which all landmarks disappear, the place beyond, and before, speech, the stage before we have returned to the marketplace, once more in deep conversation with life-as-it-is on the ground.

17. We fear to go into this silence because it feels like—and is—a kind of death. It is a numberless place and it is the first place we must inhabit on the way to the body's return to its home as the Abode of the Mother, the Hum of Shakti, which forms around itself the entire material universe, with its singleness of differences, its unity of opposites, its illuminating darkness.

18. Where is the body-as-corpse? This is not a mental exercise, some arcane practice that exists to teach us something. It is simply the truth. It is right here if we know how to look.

19. When we touch the tip of our finger to a cold piece of metal, we experience an analog of reality: We feel the coldness in the finger, though in actuality, what the finger "feels" is simply the activation and firing of a sequence of nerves. These nerves, already-in-history, that is, in the past, in reaction to what already-is,

send a message to the brain, which interprets
this feeling into already-known memories of
cold and heat, metal and glass, and sends this
impulse down to the fingertip via other nerves.

20. When this is realized, the body is seen clearly
as a mechanism, an elaborate, wonderful
mechanism, but mechanism nonetheless.

21. A machine that pretends to be alive is still
pretending. But a machine that knows itself to
be a machine is placed squarely in the real
Now, beyond the unhealed mind's hemmed-in
version of what aliveness is.

22. It is resurrected, restored, removed from
illusion. It is not sad about this. Any tears that
fall are tears of joy because the truth brings a
kind of rain that comforts all beings.

23. In searching for awakening, we are not looking
for a picture of life, but life itself, as it is. In
other words, before a return to the body-as-life
can be made, the body must recede from its
powerful position to the background, as it
were, so that another, more potent movement
can come to the fore. So that we can see that
this now we hope so deeply for, contains every
time and every thing and every when. History,
it turns out, is in the Now as well.

24. This movement allows us to see the body as a wonderful lump of clay.

25. We cannot enter this state until we have thoroughly become familiar with our historical defenses, which always seek to dissociate us from our pain.

26. Our unhealed sense of self wants to *be somebody*. But this "somebody" is an unconscious bulwark against the sea of reality. It is a construction of defenses and is not yet a real girl or a real boy.

27. The silent body, the true body of Christ before the resurrection, is not arrived at through the need for a defense, but because of the fearless stance of the warrior, who is willing to go into nothingness in pursuit of God.

28. Why "the body of Christ before the resurrection?" Because Christ's power lay in his being who he was for no other reason than being who he was, was his reason for being. It should be the same for us.

29. How do we change? We must let go of the past. To "let go" of the past means we must be willing to make enormous effort to work this

history through, to have the support to work it through, as well.

30. Letting go of the past does not mean the past no longer exists, but now it exists *as the past* and not as an echo we believe is still sounding. The past, residing in the room of our present self, is part of who we are, part of our totality but not its central part.

31. Everything becomes itself, something it always was.

32. When seen through this process, the body-as-corpse is a wonderful, freeing thing. Looking through these dead eyes at the world, we see for the first time how the truly dead masquerades as life while the dead we have found is life-in-action, each thing being itself, separate and connected to every other thing, no longer covered over in expectation, denial and hope.

33. We see around us the tragedy of life and its immediate, constant scintillation. We see the questing people, desperate for the Real, looking the other way.

34. The path to the silent body is the same as any of the paths to God: We must learn about

ourselves; we must quiet the mind; we must act
with kindness toward the self.

35. The thing that is new here is the idea that we
     are not—by doing all of this—moving toward
     some spiritually athletic vision of an "alive
     body."

36. Instead, we are looking for the body to get
     quieter and quieter, until, no longer speaking
     to us in its various tongues, the mechanism
     behind its façade of realness appears and our
     consciousness begins to see that we are the
     body but this body, in this form of the real,
     extends in all directions, humble and kind,
     limited and yet a temporary repository for the
     waves of this eternal world. This realization
     makes all the difference.

37. The bones are silent: remember this.

38. The muscles and tendons are silent: remember
     this.

39. The lungs fill and deflate. They are nothing
     but what they are.

40. The deeper we sink into things, the happier we
     are, being one with our true nature.

41.   It is paradoxical: to be alive, let the body die.
      The dead body, the silent body, is freely alive
      as the body itself.

42.   When we overeat, we are not in the silent body.
      Overeating, and every other indulgence,
      including the pursuit of pleasure, is a futile
      attempt to "stay alive."

43.   The path toward the silent body at that
      moment is awareness and immediate self-
      acceptance and forgiveness, no matter what the
      transgression.

44.   When we cannot forgive ourselves for our
      misconduct and limited self, we are in the
      conceptual body, the imaginal body, which is
      actually separate from who we are, a sort of
      idealization of what or who we think we are or
      should be. When we are in those states, we are
      not in the silent body.

45.   The silent body makes love because that is its
      nature: to join flesh to flesh; the silent body
      sings because it itself is song.

46.   Walking along the bay in Truro, I picture men
      and women with salt traps making salt from
      sea water almost two hundred years ago.

47. This same type of salt, now sold as gourmet salt called *fleur de sel*, is what everyone commonly used to salt their food until sodium chloride mines were discovered in France in the early nineteenth century.

48. Unlike *fleur de sel*, which is from sea water, sodium chloride is relatively pure. *Fleur de sel* has ten or twenty trace minerals, which have been lost in the translation to mined table salt. Boron, molybdenum, arsenic, copper, lithium, the list goes on.

49. The silent body loves the complexity of mineral rhythms. It loves the curves of arms swaying, or pelvis swaying and mouth opening and closing. It loves difference and abhors simplification, whether in medicine, politics, art, or relationship. Fascism is simple. Democracy is messy and complex. Manufactured bread turns to sugar quickly. Hand-made, whole grain bread develops slowly in the body, reducing to vitamins and minerals without danger of producing insulin-resistant, fat Americans.

50. The silent body loves nuance and subtlety. It lives in the constant life that takes place at the crossroads between things, the bazaars at the

outskirts of town, the meeting places where stories are swapped.

51. The silent body, the body that is dead to symbolic speech, can do this. It is the proper vehicle for human life.

52. The silent body learns by engaging the world and its practices. It does not learn to engage, but engages and then learns. It is not in charge of its curriculum except to show up. That is its nature.

53. To the best of its ability—since it is a limited thing—the silent body, and all of its parts, wants to do its job of living. The lungs want to breathe and transfer oxygen and carbon dioxide. The ovaries want to make eggs and the prostate fluid. The eyes want to flutter, keep moist, and see.

54. The body also wants to fall apart, because, as it is temporary, it wants to do that too. The silent body is the body in life and death.

55. The body itself is ultimately not a psychological tool. That is part of its illness.

56. It is the keeper of psychological mysteries only so far as they have not been worked through.

As they are worked through, they either leave altogether, or remain—non-symbolically, as crease or cut, bend or break, in the body proper.

57. Leaving psychology and symbolic speech behind, the body is free and then frees the mind, which is holy too.

58. Not talkative, not listening, not alive, not dead, we begin to see in the presence this silence has that it is the perfect screen for the manifestation of the Great Mother.

59. As our eyes grow dead, they open and see that all forms appear because of the Great Mother's existence. We are not filled with life, we do not contain life, but are life.

60. If we simply contained life, then upon the death of the physical body, we would lose our life forever. But dying first, we have the chance of seeing that our most essential self is the Great Mother herself. Our bodies are our Great Speech, the life we lead, Her spoken tongue.

61. No eyes, no ears, no mouth, no tongue: Giving up the pursuit of life, life comes to us. Knowing

our body is a simulacrum, we enjoy its flight
into the unknown.

62. Then when we speak, no dust comes out of our
     mouths, no moth wings, no sand. We speak
     with the tongues of angels then, which is to say,
     completely human, held as we are, in the fine
     forms of the Mother's earth.

Introduction:
Six Hymns in Spring to the Mother

It is difficult for me to communicate exactly what my relationship with the Mother is like. Let's start at the beginning.

When I first consciously decided to follow a spiritual path—although there had been inklings of it and a passion for it much earlier on—I was seventeen and reading the about the Bengali teacher Sri Ramakrishna. Sri Ramakrishna was a devotee, as I have mentioned before, of the Mother. What interested me was not so much the Mother—I wasn't sure exactly what that was—but the fact that he had understood the pure, formless unity of the nondual and *chose* to remain in a somewhat dualistic framework as a devotee of Kali, one of the presentations of the Divine Mother.

As time moved on, I continued my studies, principally in Zen and Western psychology. My entire course of study was myself. My inner suffering was great. But my will and desire to see it through, to understand and conquer it, was also strong. Everything I began to understand about the world and the people suffering in it, I understood based on this course of study entitled *myself.* And yet, even at that time, with my personality just beginning to heal, I understood that the ultimate aim of the spiritual path was not only to rectify my personal psychology but to connect with a transcendent view that, paradoxically, would allow me to be fully, and imperfectly, human.

Years later, after a long illness was resolved, I began to respond to outer requests—requests from the world and not directly from my inner sense—to create a path of healing. Whenever I "went inside" to my inner world to write, to experiment, to research and understand, I would hear a voice—it sounded like my own inner voice—telling me how to write these things down. It wasn't easy. It took thousands of pages of writing, experimental groups and most important, the constant and continuous healing of my own soul. I simply could not teach things I hadn't experienced myself.

As a poet and songwriter, I often wrote spiritual pieces. Sometimes these pieces spoke about "the Mother," but I paid little attention to that. I literally did not think about what that might mean. It was a kind of interesting split. My heart was open to this "Mother" but I didn't want to know about it consciously! For one thing, it was important for my wounded ego to believe *that it was me.* Though problematic, this was not entirely without some benefit. My inner confidence was wounded in such a way that I needed to assert my ownership of the material I was creating; I needed to gather my forces and engage the process of enlightenment directly. I also needed to find my own understanding of who and what the Mother was, and not simply take ready-made versions from others. While some thought of the Mother as the divine feminine spirit and likened her to Mother Earth and to the quality of receptivity, I knew that the Mother was something much, much more than that, and that I had to wait for it to bloom within my soul.

Over the years, I have created a new path to awakening. It always seemed to me that it was right there for the taking and that my job was mainly to heal my own broken body, mind and spirit so that I could be a vehicle for these teachings. From time to time, people would ask me if I "channeled" these teachings. I resisted that. I knew how much hard work was involved; how much suffering it took to bring this work through; efforts and failures, growth and joy, disappointment and discouragement.

But as my soul healed, I begin to understand, or let's say I began to be able to *tolerate,* the notion that none of this work belonged to me, in the same way that neither I nor any of us are responsible for any of our talents, or our breathing, our thoughts, our bodies and hopes and fears as well. This is a subtle point. It does not mean we have no responsibility: We have total responsibility. Total, but limited. In a sense, once we discover the truth, we have total responsibility to the Mother or the Universe or God or Buddha Nature—whatever you choose to call it. We have the responsibility of *letting the Mother through,* of giving voice to the biggest part of ourselves and not only our most fearful and small part. Doing this is what makes us truly alive and brings us the most possibility for true joy, intimacy and connectedness. It allows us to give in a way that does not diminish our self but in a way that lifts us up, energizes us, and makes life more vivid and alive.

In the land of true nonduality, we cannot say where the Mother resides. To say she is a separate entity is not true—useful to the ego that sees itself as *only* separate, but not true. To say this is not true, that the Mother is somehow *within us* in her entirety, is also not true because the Mother does not fit into the ego's neat world of a separate subject and object where something either belongs to us or doesn't. If we leave the realm of the subject/object split, then the Mother is in us and we are in Her simultaneously. Her Presence changes who we think we are, who we take ourselves to be. So she is separate and yet cannot be separate. We and the Mother arise together, an inseparable Whole, residing everywhere and nowhere, beyond conceptualization, beyond the small distinctions and simultaneously embedded and respectful of even the smallest separation and detail.

These poems speak to *this understanding* of the Mother. My understanding. May they spark something in you so that you hear the Mother directly, not as a subjective vision or belief or as an objective, parental being, but as who She really is.

Six Hymns in Spring
to the Mother

First Hymn

I am so happy to be healthy and alive.
I am watching the Rockaway undulate,
stepping-width wide, through the brown winter weeds
sow thistle, canary grass, shepherd's purse and
 nut sedge.
The field is managing itself,
Buddha's iron brown body laid out for me to see.
What will be the end of all of this?

In 1886, when the Master died,
his disciples allowed themselves to dream of what
 might come next.
Now that my parents are old I dream of what it will
be like when they are gone.
I am curved in the ocher grass like this river,
 unalloyed and free.
The north star swings on its pivot

holding other lights in its constellating grip
and so we get the cup that carries tears
rising in the north of the sky.

The collapse of state is its own kind of revolution.
Twilight leads to the dark. Children become old
and bend at play.
Who could have imagined all this!
I am thinking about the destruction of Jerusalem by
the Chaldeans.

From here, above the waterline, the sound
of weeping grows from its hushed beginnings
to a fierce stream-fed constant, the tone at the bottom
of every season. Even so,
the *cat's ear* blooms a yellow flower in spring,
and we have *dock weed* with its basal rosette
of wavy leaves, a plant that does not
tolerate cultivation.
And there is constant grief in the bucket of our hearts.

High in the standing-up heaven, Avalokiteshvara
Hears the sound of the lamentation of beings.
They sound like all the crickets of the world,
thousands of waterfalls falling at once,
or the aching grass bending, or the last oak leaves
rippling like paper.
And these sounds rain upward toward heaven
and bang against the windows of the house where

this Buddha lives. Avalokiteshvara is overcome.
Since his body is made of water
and this grief is rain, there is nowhere he can hide.
Its patter fills his ears.
He knows the flood that fills the land.
This is what he feels.
And he has nowhere else to go.

Second Hymn

Makes rainwater
makes lizard
makes noisy contraptions
and lightening whoop
and sear in the night sky.

Makes volcano underfoot,
melting the rubber in my shoes
makes industry and time-travel
—though we haven't proved it yet—
makes schoolchildren in black nations
and white nations, which is to say
Nigeria and Hoboken.

Makes God-is-our-doctor
Osabo in Yoruba,
and fish abundant
and fish dispersed, makes
jaguars float up from
Mexico to Arizona, scaring
and thrilling everyone because
the jaguar is a myth-evoking beast.

Makes friendships with faraway
people and friendship with some close by,
makes enemies who spit

and forget to laugh,
makes enemies who
sit at the table with you and sup.

Makes pelted-with-flowers and soft
flowers unspoken of and unseen,
and the knock of the green walnut on
the roof and the squirrel paused with
blackened self-same orb in his mouth
contemplating winter.

Made winter. Made death.
Made amnesiac child born from
the calcium of the dead, no memory
of the lineage from which he sprang.
Makes disappointment and distress,
aches like a spear in the side.

Makes the true coin that buys
attention and goods, makes gold,
makes lead. Melts lead.
Leads the blind. Makes lots of light.
Makes blossoming sounds, like explosions
of time and space, makes all that
noise and silence. Makes inflationary
universes and dark matter in the head,
all the un-thought thoughts and tumbled
street signs that help us lose our way.

We don't know where we are going:
That's You. We need help: That's You.
You are our help, our monster truck
and mantra and cycle of mathematics.
Makes you. Makes square root and
negative number. All this you kindly
give me, on this water-vapor day,
on a day filled with spirit and fog.

Third Hymn

To invent Love,
I made you,
split-fingered, hair-parted,
filled with nooks and crannies,
symbols encircling your wrists,
hanging on your neck,
two eyes which see the world
in two pieces so you can
see Me and miss Me, so you
can journey and stand still
at the same time. This
causes you pain, I know,
and I'm sorry, to lose Me
constantly amid the glare
of My effulgence, to fall
down steep ravines hidden
one step beyond the door
you thought led to Heaven.
To invent Love I had to invent
sorrow, which is to say,
invent you,
I had to create Myself,
your other half, your
partner, my own shadow
and sunlight, my outward
heart, my throbbing, my center.

Hold your hands up to me:
In this light I see the marks
on your palms,
ley-lines, light,
home.

Fourth Hymn

Mother: You are the light
of the stone and the
tool for the stone,
the edge of the curving
cloud, shaved and
sculpted in air.
You are memories
of underground passages
that were lifted up
and spoken about without
shame or fear. You
have never felt
cheated. You have
never assembled yourself
nor disassembled yourself.
You are not organized
along the patterns of weather
or daybreak or music.
You are the mixer
of letters and I see
you as a brilliant blue
spark off the park window,
glinting off a high window
near the park.
You are driving toward me
and we pass each other

by: you are driving
some place else. Stone
light and concrete light.
Light within shadows,
shadows shot
through with light.

Fifth Hymn

We are moving in
the Mother's land,
every one of us stained
with her tincture. We
would say her flesh
is abundant, folded,
dark. This is the season
of seed death. Here
we know our own
burial for the first time.
We fall apart and rise
from her igneous rendering.
Oh Mother, I was never
born and I am dead to
death, my own humus,
fetid, fertile and
abundantly alive.

Sixth Hymn

Spring opens oceans of air.
I am in an unstable time.
I stop to think about you, Mother.
I am hoping to find you again.
I am hoping to win your favor,
to hear your speech, but you
are not interested in my seductive
ways and I hardly have to listen
to hear you: you are breathing in my ear,
so there is no real story here.

A twist of green rising
from this ground is now surprisingly
covered in snow. You are
fortune itself. You are what
money was based on before
there was gold or
the exchange of goods.

I am lonely without you but
you come and go in your own
will and way. Or so it seems.
But I know you love me and
are tied to me forever so it
must be me who goes, my
feet in brown leaves or mud

or in dry or hot days,
coming and going.
You ask only one thing
of me: to praise and bless
each blessed and praised
opens two jails. I keep
expecting another message
but this is the only message
I can receive. I call you
daylight again.
I call you
moon showing itself
through fast-moving clouds
over and over again.

Introduction:
The Ever-Virgin

What is behind the myth of the virgin birth? This idea appears again and again in spiritual literature, most famously in the legends around Christ, but also in Hinduism, Sumerian, Assyrian, Babylonian, Greco-Roman and Egyptian mythology as well. When there are so many sources, there must be some underlying truth that all of these images, texts, and metaphors are trying to express.

Ecstatic speech texts are never composed from a pre-existing idea. Even the very deepest ones come from the radiant light itself, stepped-down, as it were, from Silence into words, from impression to expression. Here, we have a basic annihilation of a basic principle of cause and effect. Usually, people come from people, that is, something comes from something. Here, in the world of virgin-birth, something comes from nothing and nowhere.

This "nowhere" is really "Now here," the "now here" of shunyata, emptiness, of the Kabbalistic notion of the Ayn-Sof, "the on-going emptiness without limitation." This realm, which is actually the realm of nonduality and one that human beings already live in as the world of cause and effect as we normally think of them, is changed—changed utterly, as the poet says.

This is a poem of rejoicing. It is a way of coming home.

The Ever-Virgin

1. The ever-virgin mother is the unborn mother, the one who gives birth continuously, the one who is *mother* despite the fact She is complete unto herself, never having known *the other*.

2. There is no *other* to know.

3. When there is no *other* to know, there is silent and endless creation, unaccompanied by the cries of birth and rattles of death.

4. When there is constant virginity in the act of creation, the creative one is not changed—ever—by her exertions, but remains the field of all dreams, the enfolded place out of which all seeming dramas arise.

5. *Where are you, Mother?*

6. When we call in this way, She cannot help but answer.

7. *Will you come to me, Mother?*

8. *I am already here* is her answer.

9. She descends mountains because She comes from on high.

10. She is in the valley because She is the Valley Spirit and the richness of the earth comes from her.

11. She is filled with rays of light because She is so close to the Source.

12. She is filled with rays of light because She appears again *before the Source Itself.*

13. *Not being a person, She is beyond all persons.*

14. Being beyond all persons, She is not influenced.

15. *Being* a person, She is united with all people.

16. Being *united* with all people, She is easily influenced and waits for our questions, her answers crisp on the outer edge of her tongue.

17. She is the first ray: love.

18. She comes in a small, red dress of simple cotton.

19. She comes to protect.

20. Protect from what?

21. *From forgetting.*

22. *She is the inside of the first ray: constancy.*

23. She comes in gowns of layers of silk to help us learn to rejoice.

24. Why do we forget to rejoice?

25. We forget because we are burdened by creation itself and the things of this world.

26. Living the life of a dream, and being earnest and desiring peace, we roll our sleeves up and dig into the earth itself. Doing so, we forget other arms, other earnestness, other beauty, and the moment before heaven and earth appear.

27. She is the smile in the moon after it first appears from darkness.

28. She is the beginning of the month.

29. She is the thrust into the earth we make to hold the seed.

30. She is the reason for the seed, the smile, and the thrust.

31. We encounter the Virgin when we are small and need a mother.

32. *This is always.*

33. We encounter the Virgin when we have gone through the delta, slogging knee-high through mud and underground vines and finally coming to the sea.

34. Then, in addition to being our Mother, She is the reason the night comes and the day comes. She is the moment itself when we have already come to happiness *because there was no other place to go.*

35. When we enter happiness, we enter her land.

36. When we enter her land, we are free to be small again.

37. Being small again, we are free to free others, by reminding them they too are small, but that

they have a smile within them that is like the
first days after the new moon.

38. Oh Mother, I return to you!

39. Oh Mother, I will bow to you daily at first
     light.

40. Oh Mother, I will seek you in all women and in
     all men.

41. Oh Mother, I will try to understand your
     wisdom, which is silent, and your Creation,
     which speaks with thousands of sounds.

42. Oh Mother, I will listen!

43. Oh Mother, I will plead.

44. I will plead that all people see you shining at
     the top of a hill, that the journey up the hill out
     of ignorance be made by all people!

45. That out of despair should come illumination,
     that out of illumination should come
     dependable Silence, that out of Silence we
     should see only your face!

46. Oh Mother!

47. Oh Mother!

48. My heart has finally found you again after all these years of being a child!

49. By the faith that is in me, I promise to help you appear in the geometry of every magical night, in the straight lines of every magical day.

50. We are walking up the hill.

51. We are arm in arm.

52. She is smiling down toward us.

53. We raise our faces to catch the glory of her rain.

54. We are wet with her dew.

55. We are happy.

Introduction:
Orion's Earth

When the pieces of a puzzle come together, what is found and what is lost? For one thing, nothing is lost: all the pieces are still there; we see the edges of the individual parts. But something else is actually gained: we see the picture the parts make, a picture that might have been invisible before that moment of assembly. *Awakening* is just like this: Nothing has changed. There is still birth and death and suffering. And if anyone tells you differently, they have not yet arrived. But something is also different: We see the picture that life is making moment by moment. Instead of only being overwhelmed by pieces and edges, we see at last the great *mandala* that the pieces are part of. Once that is seen, other, deeper qualities can come into play. Where before there was only color, or shape or line, now there is flow, and rhythm and emptiness and fullness and people, scenes, trees and water.

This next piece arose as I had a moment of trying to convey the interpenetration of things, this view of the world when things "appear distinct while not being separate."

Finally, this excerpt from the *Brihadaranyaka Upanishad*, an Indian Vedic text, one of the earliest examples of examination of the nondual. It leaves the world of theory and catches the wind of the actual, which is to say, why all of this matters:

> *Now this self, verily, is the world of all beings. In so far as he makes offerings and sacrifices, he becomes the world of the gods. In so far as he learns (the Vedas), he becomes the world of the seers. In so far as he offers libations to the fathers and desires offspring, he becomes the world of the fathers. In so far as he gives shelter and food to men, he becomes the world of men. In so far as he gives grass and water to the animals, he becomes the world of animals. In so far as beasts and birds, even to the ants, find a living in his houses, he becomes their world. Verily, as one wishes non-injury for his own world, so all beings wish non-injury for him who has this knowledge. This, indeed, is known and well investigated.*

Orion's Earth

On the back of my hand, in front of my eyes, I see the signs of all of the times.

From a distance, the rabbit comes, from a controlled environment, perhaps a park, a copse of trees, now into the field, the high amber grass. So did yesterday arrive in a swirl of tomorrows: The sun and moon mixed together as if they were one thing. We see the folds of the gown in the painting and it looks so real. It is all different shades of white that give things depth. What was I thinking?

From a distance, the rabbit comes. Oh yes, the ancient pulse is in me again. It's as if the booming footsteps of anything small fill everything. The air is mixed with time. The scent of the ocean, a bit of perfume on your skin, the waves velcroed to your dreams.

Continuous sunlight creates a glass. Trees are hyphenated by glimpses of something real.

Conversation seems important at the time. Soon you disappear and the leaf shakes in the real wind.

Speaking of this leaf: it is a Buddha there to enlighten you. There is nothing you need do but pay attention to this leaf. Chlorophyll. Green dust. Algae. Minnows of white light.

What is the perspective you are trying to arrange? The body is a syntax with rules and longings. The eyes are a context and make the luminous touch. The pigs are in the pen because we don't want them to go anywhere. Starlight, expanding in all directions, universes away, saves some ray to hit our eyes so gently. We don't notice our starlit arms.

On the back of my hand, in front of my eyes, I see the signs of all of the times past and future. The restaurant I wanted to go to is closed. Another has taken its place. It has a patio of glazed stones, over-hanging trees and a small courtyard where occasionally men come and go and has the sort of green haze you associate with the everglades though we are far north.

There is something in the field. I can tell because the grass moves in the air, the stalk heads describing small circles. This goes on in a straight line as something comes toward me, something invisible but quite tame, I'm sure. Really, I am waiting for it all to happen.

Once we throw ourselves off this band of air we cease doing commerce. We get out of the habit of spending. There is no other way around it. We find it hard to make connections, but everything beckons.

And birds find us first. Then the gauze of leafy things. Then the melodies of voices, snatches of conversation, a bit of putting two and two together. There is Rigel-light on the back of your hand, the leg of the giant brushes by you, striding boroughs at a time. We are amused. We forget to breathe in a moment like this, but then something reminds us and we breathe again.

Introduction:
Tefillin Psalms

When we understand the true nature of prayer it reveals itself to be a nondual process, a way of relating to the universe from the perspective of "things appearing distinct while not being separate." Let me explain.

In the usual mode of prayer, we ask for something and hope to receive it. Or, we acknowledge our gratefulness for something...to "someone."

In this understanding of prayer, there is dualism-within-dualism, which is to say, a separation between subject (the prayerful one) and the object (the One we are praying to...however we see that...). We can look at prayer—and even actualize it—from an entirely different understanding, however, one in which duality is simply a feature of the Great Unity and not something essentially separate.

Inherent in the usual form of prayer is that we need to do something (pray the right way; say the right words; adhere to the ritual; be a good enough 1) person, 2) monk, 3) father, mother, sister, brother...and so on; you get the idea) in order for something to occur. The fact of the matter is: if being any of these things is what it takes to get our prayers answered, *we can never achieve anything!* If we are honest with ourselves, we see that we are basically imperfect beings who can never really "earn" anything. Instead, anything we receive must come from the motherly love that gives simply because we exist. At the same time, we never will know when prayer works or not—or why.

But when prayer conforms to the *only thing that we are truly capable of*—honesty—then prayer *does work*. We can feel it. Something profound and deep changes within our own body and soul. *We* change, and we begin to feel this fatherly/motherly love that is given gratuitously, which is to say freely and for no reason. Honesty seems to be the way to open this door that is never actually closed.

I have practiced this form of prayer for many years and these Psalms are one of the products. They came at a time of deep struggle for me, struggle with the theistic way itself and personal struggle. But it was *honesty* that I fell back upon when all else had failed—or seemed to fail. In these prayers, I was not afraid to say anything—anything at all, as long as it was the truth of the moment. I knew that impeccable adherence to the truth of the moment, where I was from moment to moment, would lead me home. I knew within my own heart, that my Jewish roots could be reconciled with my nondual understanding and that the act of prayer itself, *prayer as process,* would create its own map or resolution, that it would result in a settling into the Great Faith. If these psalms are worth reading, they are worth reading because they are totally honest and written in such a way that if you read them and find your own honesty within them, your prayers will be answered too. The gateless gate will open for you as it did for me.

These are called "tefillin psalms" because I wrote these prayers when I was putting on *tefillin* or phylacteries as part of my morning meditation practice. These prayer-objects are aids that a person puts on their body with intricate windings and knots that emulate specific Hebrew letters; they contain prayers written on tiny parchment, which embody the truth of the Unity of God or Reality. To me, this truth, stated in the Jewish tradition, is no different from the Buddhist notion of the *Dharmakaya*, the true motive force of the universe.

Each day or so, one of these psalms would come. My job was to answer the calling of each one with complete honesty, knowing that even the most dense aspect of my personality, when revealed, would lead me—right in the psalm itself—to move from despair to joy, from confusion to clarity in my purpose, hope and happiness.

Please pick one of these psalms per day and try to live with its message during the day. Find *its* truth in *your* truth.

Live freely.

Tefillin Psalms

1.

Today I look for You
in Darkness,
Today I sing to You in Silence,
You say yet another Word;
You say, I am Here Always.
With no flashing there is flashing
with no correction there is turning
with no direction there is a center.
Oh God, I am learning to unbridle my Heart
from the concepts of good and bad,
small and large. Then You appear,
leaping, and my still heart falls
beating before Your onslaught.

2.

Between the doorways of Past and
Future, there is a corridor to You,
Excellent One:

Within the voices of the very old,
within the voices of the very weak
at the moment of dissipation
into Nothing, a kind of singing
emerges.

Help me break free.
Bind my arm
anoint my head
and let Your crown fall upon me.
I know how to use it now,
after many years of wandering.
If I grow taller, I can reach Heaven,
Your Ear and Your Eye are everywhere.
You are grainy Reality in my mouth
and my mouth Itself.

Do not suggest another route to You:
I'm coming by the most direct path.

3.

I did not see You in the
middle of the room
and things came apart.
I felt awkward and cramped
and You could not flow in.
Ageless One, are You
Listening to me, standing
off in the shadows
immersed in Your Robe?
Then Victory came and
like a spear, pierced
my separateness, and
Splendor arrived, and
You filled the room with Light,
rising inch by inch.
Air and ceiling
floor and earth,
and fire in between.

4.

If I need to bear this pain
let me fill it with water
and float on it.
If I need to sink in it,
let my lungs be huge and
my breath deep and long
and let me dive to the bottom.
If I must drown in it,
Dear God, let me swallow
as much of it as I can
and sink to You quickly,
rapid as a heartbeat
in a bird sensing danger.
If nothing like this is to happen,
and I am making too much of it,
and I am to walk, step-by-step
toward You, may I see
the water and the breath and the bird
as my illusions, and the pain I
bear as my ticket home.

5.

I know I am not so bad
but I hit my head over and over again.
I know that I am not so lonely,
yet tears of rage and acid
fall from my fingertips.

I know I am one among many,
yet I try to be Your only son.
Why do I turn the daytime
into my own private night?
I know I am continuous in Your Eyes,
but I feel in pieces in my own small heart:
Why, oh why have I not
picked up the telephone to call You?

My tefillin wraps around my arm,
Your Word sits on my heart and head,
Life within me pulses wildly,
Yet I often wish that I were dead.

Oh God let me enter the cave of Unknowing
Oh Body let me walk on the waters of bliss.
Oh God help me put the Signs together,
So that I won't slip into
confusion.

Heaven becomes hell in an instant of forgetting.
And hell is not so bad when I remember
that finding and losing
are brothers.

6.

Dear God, I sincerely
don't want
to fix myself
up,
to live another day without You,
to put myself together again
and sincerely believe my confusion.

Dear One of Many, and Many One,
Dear Hope and Loss, Dear Sorrow and Sleeping,
Dear Small Advances, Dear Large Thought,
I hold Your hand and I sing to You.

In the middle of the violence of
the sun is Light,
In the middle of absence
is calm, tender, night.
In the middle of apprehension,
is a steady Light.
In the middle of *nega* is Delight.

Walking with You.
Walking with You.
Walking with You.

7.

A prayer can keep me from You,
a mistake,
a house of prayer can keep me
from Home,
a song make me miss You.
Searching for Your Trail,
I miss You in the Sky,
and looking in the clouds, I might
not hear Your Mouth filled
with warm earth speaking.
Sometimes Silence is best,
and Your words wrapped
around my arm melt into
my bones and flesh and become Me.
Oh God, there is one air and
there is another: one goes in
and the other out.
Over and over again I think of
You...

8.

I start out stiff
with dreams, my body
in another time and place,
and I say, "Thank you
for waking me up into
this world once again,
Your faithfulness is great, "
and I feel my jaw and my
feet hurt with where I've
stepped and what I've said.
By the time I read "Oh Listen,"
I am beginning to hear, and my
body sways and dips a
little into Your World.
At the "Blessed are You,"
my ankles proclaim their
innocence, my heart
lowers itself by itself,
and the letters begin to
flash on the page. My eyes
say, "What is it, this
brightness in the middle
of the world?"
It is only then I see You
sitting with me, sitting in me,
writing words and singing songs.
How long can I go on?

ECSTATIC SPEECH

Each moment of the morning prayer
makes me more alive.
I can't bear it.
So I finally stop, afraid
to find out what will
happen if I walk off
the end of
the world.

9.

The Light whispers
and weaves on my sunlit floor.
Soft leaves bend it,
and it scours the floor like honey.
Oh marry me, God,
and call the ceremony my Life.
A lifetime of food,
many voices of friends,
white clothing,
childhood and old age...

I hear Your Music
and I try to bend like honey and leaves
but I am unable.
But God, I am slowly becoming Lighter,
and then You can bend me!

10.

I see Your Light in my daughter
and my daughter's Light in You.
Her sweet thinking is like Yours
when you created the World.
Her movement toward subtlety
is sure, as when you gave
Abraham the Ram.
Her Light must be pleasing to You,
like a sweet fragrance in a
forest after a rain, rising up
and renewing You.
It must remind You of why
You made us: for the pleasure
of smell and thought, fine
heart and sacred body.
I watch her daily finding You
in all the decisions she makes:
to stand for this,
to be against that,
to go there,
to not go there.
She is molding her form in
Your image
and when I look up at You
I see her sweet smile
on Your Lips...

11.

Oh Life, let me find You
hidden in the bulrushes
of good and bad,
floating on the water
in a small chamber,
reached for, lifted
and caressed, a foundling
in a princess' arms.
Oh Life, let me hold You,
exquisite detail in a
viney leaf, the wind
trapped and singing in
a reed.
Oh Life, let me enjoy you:
wherever You carry me
I am on Your River, and
willing to go.
Though I go down to Death,
I am with You, silver,
silent, never alone.

(With the arm tefillin I bind
my left and right sides together:
with Your Name on my Head
I stand straight, no matter
where I walk...)

12.

With the two wings of
my *tallis*
I enwrap
One Bird.
With One Body
I fly over the World.
I see Your Light Everywhere.
With flaming fringes,
the World is decorated:
many flowers, many forms.
Snapping turtles in the pond
biting and making Love.
Enwrapped in Hod, I sparkle,
reflecting Your Will
that I should be Myself.
Being Myself, I love You,
and You call back to me:
Bird! Bird!
The Voice that made the World
twittering, a series
of whistling sounds and always
air, rushing in
and out.

13.

Today I understood
the tefillin are a kind
of One, and the
black binding straps
hold me down to the earth
as a kind of sacrifice.
I am held to the altar of
What Now? and When?
Between the horns of past
and future, I lie stunned
by Your Kindness.

What of the Blood? And
the smell of Death?
I am Isaac, bound
to be Free, awaiting
A Ram who waits to take my Place.

And a Bird takes the Ram's Place,
and an Ant, the Bird's,
and a Plant, the Ant's
and a Leaf, the Plant's,
which finally swirls
in this storm of Human Life.

I unwrap this Leaf and on it
write Your Name
and it is taken up by the Wind
You Made,
the One that waits for us All.

14.

Once in the evening I followed
You until only Your Footsteps
were left in the Dark.
I followed You further until
the night wore away any sound
and only the rhythm of when Your steps
might fall was left.
I went further, beyond rhythm,
beyond night.
I found You standing in the middle of
the Darkness that does not need night to be,
that only needs the Space to breathe.
Then, no more walking.
No more echoes of footfalls.
No more searching for Your Face:
You were There, like a round piece of tar
on a macadam road, blackest black on black,
Essentially Good.

15.

Life is long when
we are awake
and when we are asleep,
as swift as the cry of
a night-hooded hawk.

In the pond turtles play.
Something makes a wave
and breaks the surface of the stillness.
For years, the sunlight pushes
against each tree's trunk and makes
even the biggest of them
eventually lean.
Oh God, if I could
go back to the days my
wife carried our daughter
around on her chest,
my daughter's golden hair...
Slowly cherishing the flight
of the pendulum as it
swings through Life
toward Infinity....

Where are You Oh Lord,
when we are asleep?
Growing the vineyards.
Preparing the wine.
Carrying us close to
Your Heart.

16.

Since I am not the target
of anyone's dreams,
I am here with You.
Since I am not the target
of my parents' pain,
I spend time with You.
Since no one is in the way
of my speech, since my
speech is not used like a weapon,
You appear to take me to lunch.
Since I am willing to be quiet,
You speak, and my
Whole World comes
into Being.

17.

Let my body be
Let my body be open
Open to receive Your Good
Open from chest to belly.

Let my body be soft,
let my body be singing,
filled to the brim with the Light You Bring
Oh Holy One of Whom I am a Part.

Let me honor this flesh,
and not despise it by declaring it worthless
and look the other way
when I am contained in such Beauty.

Let my body be,
let my body be truly my own,
forgoing history and other's hands,
and receive instead from Your Heart
wet dew from an untouchable cloud.

Oh God, You gave me this body
in order to Praise You.
It is Praise that makes this flesh
hang like a story on a page of bone.

18.

I am married to Life:
It cannot be otherwise.
All my distance before
was my difficulty with the Real.

I am married to Life:
I wear Life's triple ring
around my finger:
for my honeymoon I live on Earth,
forgoing the *Gan Eden*
for the flesh and blood of others.

I am married for life,
never to part until my
breath disappears.
And even after, in those
continuous moments of
non-breathing Splendor,
while my Spirit returns to Heaven,
I will feed fish and birds
in the small budding creatures
who sparkle and glisten
and live.

19.

I won't be so presumptuous
as to call You when You
don't call me,
but I think I hear a bell
ringing.

I will be so tall as to
look over my shadow so that
I can see Your Sunlight.
I won't be a liar and say
I won't be frightened again.

But God, something has happened:
I have begun the prayer of
sacrifice and the Temple
has appeared.
I have asked for an Altar
and You have given me the World.
All my life I
have searched for
Infinity, hoping it
would carry me
past Death.

Now I know it is every-moment-
dying that will
bring me to Life,

and make my dry
bones young again,
and my face filled
with Spirit.

And like Water escaping,
uncontained in my cupping hands,
I find myself again,
here
in the glistening rocks.

20.

The unwelcome traveler
arises at dusk, and
it gets darker.

And all the seasons under
his foot, crushed
like sand or fireflies.

I try to understand
but fail. I try
to question but there is

no echo.
I try to light the Back
to see the shape of the

Front, but there are
only shadows. Then
You come, Lord,

Striding like daylight.
First it is dawn, then
it gets Lighter,
and suddenly I see
my hand in Yours
and I am joined to

ECSTATIC SPEECH

Life again, as if
I had never been
apart.

21.

Putting on a pair of new tefillin,
praying for a friend.
"May she put on a new skin,"
winding down the arm
like a stairway from Heaven
to Earth.
"May she recover,"
a new way,
an afternoon prayer,
something to say.

What is in these little boxes?
They are closed, so no one
knows.
How much liberation?
How much freedom?
How much sorrow and joy?
Her body is unwinding its black straps,
down into darkness it goes:
May she be in Light.

22.

God, I cannot say, "God."
Force of the Universe,
I cannot commit You to memory,
work You into a story
or song, imagine You,
think of You, handle or
hold You.

God of the Universe, You
have disappeared into the
wind and rain and summer.
You do not notice me,
but only the Uncreated in me,
the one who is Whole Forever.

Depressions in the earth fill
with water.
Sides of mountains generate
wind and steam from rain.
Everything feels its
purpose
because of what it is.

You flow into the anointed hollow
of my hand,
and You fill my waiting heart.

TEFILLIN PSALMS

(Someday my heart will disappear,
and You will flow around
the space I used to be...)

23.

The *Shema* is a living creature
with eyes everywhere,
with beaks and wings,
arms and legs, a tender
look, a brown eye.

The *Shema* is a chariot
and I climb into it,
it climbs into me,
and we go everywhere
together.

Oh Great Listening, you have
become Silence, and all
Your Sounds fit in
one Cup, one Place.
I watch every tree
on the hillside wave
with one wind.
My arms wave too,
hello and goodbye.

24.

Dear God, let me calm
down. Irritable soul,
world-cornered, leavened too
high or not leavened enough,
I am showing my true devil
nature, the killer
who seeks control and a
smooth life.

Dear God, teach me not
to be calm, hiding my
irritable soul under
hardened lava, strange,
smooth black rock.

Let me be more like You,
volcanic but kind,
irritable but industrious
to make repair.
Let me have the energy
to go through the world
making it
Whole.

25.

Black winding straps
don't hold bone and
flesh together:
they hold the spirit
to the bone.

26.

Flash of Abraham:
black fire.
Flash of Isaac:
black fire.
Flash of Sara:
black fire,
and Rachel
and Rebecca:
black fire.
Flash of Jacob:
black fire.
I am part of a people
who have ridden
black fire from
Sinai to the Present.
I am going back
to that small Place
in the desert,
where it all began.

27.

Finger
wrist
arms
biceps
heart
body
head
nape
of
neck.
The Complete Man.

28.

To have conditions right
(To need no conditions at all)
to have the straps wound tightly
(to see You when they loosen and fall)
to remember You when I think of You
(to remember You when I don't think of You)
to insist that You take me high on
Your Chariot, to plead with You
that I am Ready
(To leave everything to You, to
take what You give me).

This is my life: two hands,
two legs, two arms, two feet.
(And all of it alights in
Heaven.)

29.

Good to return to Your Womb
again: soft again,
my hand held up to greet
and not protect.

Good to see great things

in every package, Your
Holy Sparks in every color
from gray to impossible to say.

We are commanded not to
cook a kid in its mother's milk:
This is because
Your Milk must remain
forever kind to us, a Place
of Refuge from the heat
of learning. You are leaning
into me, Shoulder to shoulder.

Today there is rain all
over the world.
I prepare to coil myself
around You, and You prepare
to wrap Yourself around my arms,
gently, as a Mother enfolds her Child.

30.

You enter me with
a bit of murmuring air,
and I don't know which is more
difficult: to be with You or
without You.

There is a steel in me
that insists,
a metal hook that catches
on my sleeve,
a meaning that eludes me,
a face that will not
face me,
but I am compelled toward
You like a planet in a gravity-well,
no mind but falling,
no thought but "go there."

ECSTATIC SPEECH

Oh Lord,
reduce my fear.
Let me go
to my obvious
conclusion.
I've turned around
You all my life
and I know the
next here
is already
Here.

31.

Nothing I can say
does not hold my history.
To speak to You is
to fall unconscious.
So I will keep Silent.

To say Nothing and forget
about my past makes
a new place for evil
to dwell, so I must speak.

Oh pain: I gather
you into Silence. I
keep you with me,
lit and bright, and read
my Silence by Your
Lamp and find,
as the Darkness melts,
the One sits with me
at my table,
listening to the
Real Thing we
cannot talk about.

32.

You show up
with a cake
we can eat together
and my mind goes
out the window.

Thought dies
slowly, and it's a
difficult death.

But then I am free
to roam from room
to room

Until I finally come to
the kitchen. There You are
sitting at the table
Smiling at me.

You hand me a piece of cake
and we smile together,
the Two of Us, eyes rolled upward
with Sweetness on
the tips of our tongues.

33.

Front to back
let Your Life
penetrate me.

From my beginning to my end
let me be in Your grip
happy to pull my humanity
to a Larger Place.

At the final inches
of the race, we slow
down: the dream of moving
through thick glass or water
takes over: We cannot move.

Heal me through these
final feet: move me through
this place if it takes one hundred years.
Encourage me from the sidelines,
call to me from the finish line.

Only You will
satisfy me, You and the
sound of Your Voice.

34.

For my Pleasure and Yours
there is a certain way of doing things,
and I read the Beginning and I read the End.

And when the Gates open,
and when the Center opens
and when the day brings Light
and the night, Darkness,

When, according to Plan
things perish in goodly time,
neither hurried nor held back,
then Your Pleasure increases and
mine does too.

Lord, this is the story of our lives here on Earth.
Help me find the Torah in my cells
so that my entire body unfurls into You.
Uncoil my Heart,
let it be Plain.
Let each beat be
a single black letter in Your Book of Certainty.

May the words of my mouth
and the meditations of my heart
be acceptable to You, O Faithful Friend
and Compassionate
Reader of my Soul.

Introduction:
The Pleasures of a Moral Life: Hedonism and the Bodhisattva Way

Masquerading as an essay, this discussion of the Bodhisattva way is also meant to take you step by step into a fresh and new perspective of what so-called *awakening* is about.

The old Zen adage *three years to satori, thirty years to enlightenment,* is true. Satori is the spice that entices your tongue. Enlightenment, much less flashy, is cooking in the kitchen, inviting people over for dinner and enjoying the feast.

This piece describes the step-by-step journey you are already on. The awakening mind, unlike a mind that thinks it is "awakened" once and for all, is fluid and changeable. But this inclination toward fluidity is not vacillation or lack of commitment: it is commitment to the Real Self that you do not own and yet have never given up.

The Pleasures of a Moral Life: Hedonism and the Bodhisattva Way

You decide—through the practice of some introspective technique or some momentary but pervasive thought—that what "you" are is nothing personal; that the personal itself is a masquerade for...what? You cannot yet decide. But it seems to you that this "personal self," something so close as to be all but invisible, begins to reveal itself as a kind of shorthand for a particular point of view rather than an actual thing. You realize, to use a physical example, such as height or eye color, that you cannot take credit for having blue eyes or being five-foot nine: to do so would be absurd. Indeed, you see that "you," this *personal person*, did not invent anything at all, even your ability to think about these things, though you cooperate with the urge to think them.

In fact, you realize that *taking credit* for those things—believing that they are something "you" have accomplished—would be a form of slavery and that you are better off—much better off—realizing that they are the result of forces that are *not you*, impersonal forces, and that the *you* that is created from them is only a shell for something else; that to identify with it as a "real something," lacks insight into the way things actually are. It's as if an eddy in the river, in a moment of self-reflection, realizes it is not something autonomous and separate, though it does have its own capacities, shape and dynamics, but is principally *the river in a different and temporary form.*

You continue with your introspective journey and discover that you cannot take credit for your ideas, or talents, or even your emotional state of being. True, you have *responsibilities* toward them, for instance, to develop your talents, to make choices that further your goals. But these are all after-the-fact things: In all of the basic matters, you had virtually no say.

Again, you discover that instead of leading to nihilistic feelings, you feel liberated, as strange as that seems. Realizing the truth of this, you no longer have any territory to protect and therefore can instead interact with the world freely and creatively. Life becomes more fun. Things flourish. This is the beginning of the stage of the "wise and foolish being."

You start looking at your actions and begin seeing that most of them can be categorized as "actions-for-the-good." You are not sure why this is so. Though you think of yourself as a good person, having this freedom should allow you to do *anything*, anything good *or* bad. Instead, what seems to give you the most pleasure are actions that help others in some way. Even the very act of *relating* seems to bring this pleasure.

You realize that this is not *self-less*: it is actually *self-full*. It enlarges the self, but a different type of self than you would be enlarging if you had to protect the territory you thought you had invented yourself.

But now, in the present incarnation of your thinking, realizing that you have no territory that you yourself created and nothing or at least little to protect, the self that enjoys this way of being seems to be a different type of "self." You wonder what to call it.

And then you think: *All of my actions seem to draw their being from a similar moral place. They are all water from the same well.*

This makes you wonder about morality.

You realize that when you had territory to defend, your morality came from the outside, whether it was thinking of other thinkers, or from some concept of what is good or bad. You could even say that your morality came from *your thinking.*

You begin to understand that when you have no territory to defend even your thinking process has changed. It still goes on, but sometimes you notice that there is no "watcher" of these thoughts. Then they go on like springtime, with no need of a "you." Yet, "you" continue to enjoy these moments. Thinking in this way goes on, in other words, but it is a display, useful, interesting, helpful...but also not "you."

Then returning to morality, you wonder what type of morality exists that *does not* come from the first type of thinking—that is, when your moral thoughts were protective of your own space or sense of internal shape. You wonder if there is an "objective morality." And if there is, you wonder if—despite the fact it is called "objective," it is the same for all people.

This leads you to the thought that from this enlarged position, the position that is beyond this earlier form of thinking, wherein you have no territory to defend, no self in the usual sense to defend, exactly what the term "other people" actually means.

If you see yourself one way when you are in a territorially defensive position, and you see yourself in an entirely different way when you are no longer taking "credit" for who you are, that you have, in other words, deferred to some other power as the maker of you, whether that other power is spiritual or scientific, then perhaps the way you see other people and even the world has changed as well.

You ask yourself the question: *Why do I choose to do the things I do? What makes them mine?* And you realize that that is the wrong question with which to begin your journey to understanding this question. You think: *perhaps these things I do, these things that seem "moral," that seem to give me pleasure; that the world takes as "altruistic," or the signs of a "good and moral person," are actually not mine either!* This is a startling thought: that there is a type of moral action that you do but which does not arise from the "personal self" as you formally understood it.

Then what is morality that is not yours and simultaneously is not imposed from the outside? Is it real? Is it significant?

You continue to think about this and you entertain the thought that perhaps this form of morality *is the only real morality* and this leads you to try to understand what you mean by "real."

Is it "real" as in "I can touch it?" or "I can think about it?" or "Other people see this too?" You are amazed as all of these categories drop away—since you are no longer "thinking" the way you once did, and you are left with a sense of the real that is not dependent upon anyone else's thinking, but is *connected* nonetheless, *with everything.*

Your sense of freedom increases. Now you are connected but not imprisoned; part of, but free. Now you are free to be limited—as you actually are—as a finite human being and yet, somehow simultaneously, something more. You can sense it, just beyond your arm's reach...

Are morality and pleasure somehow united? This seems like a dangerous idea, a license somehow to be hedonistic. But maybe you've misjudged hedonism in its highest form. Perhaps you've only thought of hedonism like someone who thinks they are "a person," someone who has taken credit for their life as their own invention. But what of a new type of hedonism, one that you inhabit *after* you realize that you cannot take credit for anything in your life that is primary; that your "credit," or effort, is limited to secondary affairs—important, but not the main event.

Now hedonism becomes another display—as thinking did. You are free of it, yet connected to it, just as your actions seem to be altruistic, but are equally connected to your own pleasure, the pleasure of a free man or woman who has no territory to defend.

You begin to understand that morality's root is not in the emotional or rational body, that instead of being a "code," it can be described anew as "the way the world likes to work because it works better that way and is more enticing..." The world, our world, the entire world of manifested beings, shy, coy, fetching, blatant, colorful, dark, light and vitally alive, likes to be that way...

What a strange thing to say and what a strange way to put a philosophical position! Yet, you feel drawn to this perspective.

Rivers like to flow. "Like," when taken personally, means you are anthropomorphizing the river. But when taken from this new perspective, "like" is an appropriate word: hydrogen atoms "like" oxygen atoms. That is the way the world works best for all concerned, from galaxies to fish to you and me.

Plants depend upon a cycle of rain and dry weather. We eat plants. Eating, we live. Living, we think. Even thinking we are a *personal-person* is a kind of glory, the light of which cannot be seen while we are still attached to the position of being a separate person as an absolute-and-only-truth. And on it goes.

So perhaps "morality" can be understood in a new way too, as something we personalize, and therefore make moral judgments about and discuss and think about, but really, underneath, something that arises naturally because it is an expression of the way the world works most economically. And the world loves the principle of least effort. It is Grace Itself.

Following your own heart, you do certain things and reject others. As you continue your journey of "not-owning," you seem to reject more things of a certain type, things that come from the outside, that are someone else's thoughts and ideas. You begin to trust your own "non-thinking/thinking mind" to guide you to work in the way the world works, which is to say, more easily and with more pleasure, more *morally*, if you would like to put it that way.

You derive even more pleasure thinking about this in this way and become a boon to the world, a bodhisattva whose mission is based on abundance

and clear seeing and not on deprivation and denial;
on something that frees and does not encumber.

Introduction:
The Barking Saint

I've left the Barking Saint for last. What is there to say about an intruder who makes himself at home, sits at your table and eats your dinner, retires to your bed and won't leave the house? At first, I tried to ignore him. I thought if I didn't cooperate— and I didn't even know what he wanted!—he would leave out of boredom or disgust with my recalcitrance. But it didn't happen. After years of being bothered by him, I began to pay attention.

I found him inconvenient. He always pointed out—in the nicest way, you understand—my inconsistencies, selfishness and inauthenticity. But little by little, I began to count on him to tell me the truth when I couldn't tell it to myself. I even found myself missing his voice when he would not speak, missing his presence when he seemed to go on vacation.

I deeply understood that though he can be crude and rude, he has the kindness of stones and rivers in him and when he disappears like daylight melting into night, he also always appears as day when night melts away. He leaves only to return again.

I asked him one day if he was the *only* Barking Saint. He looked at me like I was an idiot. I've learned to unfurl his remarks and looks and this is what he meant to say—if he only had good manners:

There is a Barking Saint in each sentient being. He (or she) is the spirit that guards the real self, the authentic one beyond characteristics, who sits, no matter what damage life brings, in each being, waiting to be called upon. When called upon, this saint is the genius of soul and the sound of his voice wakes your heart.

There is no question in my mind that you have a barking saint within you at this very moment, waiting to come out.

The Barking Saint

1.

By Way of Shaking Your Hand

Some of this is fat and the rest of it is lazy.

Some of it may bring you comfort, but much of it is
simply a waste of time and you'd be better off
reading the paper.

Some of it is exciting: that's the worst part: it may
send you off barking at night, or stopping the odd
person on the street and with deep sensitivity,
satisfaction and a profound sense of peace, smelling
their ass.

2.

Throw out the ego.

No. Bring it back again.

Throw out the ego, the one who looks at everything twice and sings about what's left.

No. No. No. Bring back this mirror that looks at everything twice and look at everything twice: everything is beautiful and deserves a second look.

Throw out all notions of separateness or lightness or darkness and exist in the web of beginninglessness and endlessness and all that.

OK: No! No! No! Be separate! Hold out your hand! Greet the Great Thing who has come to visit!

For the last time: throw out all your notions, the mother you carry around, the father in your pocket, your male pelvis, your female chest, your links with the past, your history-stubbled face, your atonement, your lies, your inspiration, hesitation, confusion and tears.

Absolutely for the absolute last time: No! No! No! Take it all back. If you can't find all you've lost over the years or mistakenly given away, steal it. Invent it. Remember it. Love it.

3.

The head of the flower forms its eyes. For a while it
looks out at the world. Soon it drops and discovers
its body, long stem, leaves, and it feels its roots for
the first time, sucking liquid rock from some
endless place.

Then it notices the weather. Wet like fall, hot like
summer, or cold like winter. Through the weather it
discovers time and with that notion playing in its
head it begins to look more carefully around. But by
this time, its eyes are failing. And through this
failing it begins to understand something.

This understanding descends like sap to the rest of
its body, through its roots down into the endless
place. It says, "This place is not endless. It clearly
ends. I'm falling apart."

The endless place continues to sleep.

Then the flower says, "I am connected to this place,
yet I am disappearing and this place remains. But
what is this place without me? How is all this
possible? Won't you speak to me?"

The endless place says, "How is that possible?" like
an echo.

The flower droops lower and lower and a few leaves begin to decay. Some of the roots soften and lose their focus.

Watching a leaf drop from its body, the flower sees it decay into dirt, and within a short time, part of itself is indistinguishable from the endless place.

The endless place looks back up at the flower.

The flower looks down at the endless place.

Everything is said in that instant, and it is like a new season, one that no one ever heard of before.

A crown forms on the head of the earth, and like a diadem it shines and shines.

4.

On Monday I was sitting on a rock. This rock was
my heart and Monday was my soul. It was a pale,
sandy-colored rock, ancient of history and firm of
feeling: it did not fall easily into something else, but
kept its shape and its idea of who it was in grasp.

Monday was another story: It moved from rock to
rock, lifted up its neck to look over the trees and
bushes to see what it could see. It was always
looking. It was as quick as the rock was slow,
excitable as the rock was calm. Together, they made
a good pair, Monday jumping from rock to rock
and the rock accepting it all, bemused, thinking
slowly of sometime in the future, but not there yet.

Why do I tell you this story? Because your
happiness depends upon it. Without Monday, the
rock might become lava, and have little time to
contemplate eternity. Without the rock, Monday
would become stolid, fixing itself precisely, stopping
the wheel of the week forever.

Some parts of us are rocks and some parts days and
some parts water and some parts weeping. It's hard
to make sense of it all, but so it goes.

So my advice is: Stand on your rock and crane your
neck. If you look carefully, you can just see the rings

of water moving out from where a fish just jumped
from invisibility to invisibility again. Tell your story
about this to everyone you see: They might be
interested.

5.

Where does the melody come from?

It comes from the forehead.

Where does the wilderness in the melody come from?

It comes from Michael, who lives in Heaven.

Where does Heaven begin?

For us, when we sing.

When we sing, the world within us falls silent and we begin to hear Your Voice.

What does Your Voice sound like?

Like noise. Like seltzer. Like lizards. Like time. Like butchers. Like lime. Like shade.

If we get small enough, can we fit into this Silence and will it carry us away?

No.

Why not, if every moment of God is a boat and if God wants us and sends us a messenger or conveyance?

Because.

Because why?

Because why.

This is the reason Heaven and Earth are separate.

Let me tell you a story:

Once upon a time someone swallowed "why" and there was no why in the world. Now a world without why may seem like a good thing, but it is not. When we ask "why is it raining?" we learn about clouds and weather. When we ask, "Is this safe to eat?" we learn about cuisine and spices. In this way we learn the world, and God wants us to learn about the world: we are here for that purpose. But once we learn the world, we might want to learn something else. After all, we are creatures whose curiosity knows no bounds. But now, at this new frontier of knowledge, "why" is not the key and is not the tablet nor is it the pen or the ink. So "why" becomes our lock, our shutting the door of something new in our own faces. Swallowing "why" becomes everybody's business at some time in their lives. When we finally swallow "why" we follow the word down past our own tongues into our own throats and into our own bellies. We become a shade, a

shadow that passes for a human being but which is
something else: a miracle.

Now small enough, we see where the melody came
from: it came from the forehead where all the
thoughts that love the world and God came from.
And then we wonder: where did the forehead come
from?

We wonder all of this aloud and then you might say
we are in Heaven, singing.

6.

One day it was a bad day. It was difficult to find my footing. I walked into every situation like I was walking on wet stones hidden under rushing water. My foot disappeared into the stream, touched something solid for a moment, and then I tumbled. I had to save myself time and again.

This made me despair.

7.

I have nothing to note. The day is somewhat gray and it is after a storm. The pond is full after being empty for so long, but the water is muddy and the grass is slick with water that still rises up from the soaked ground. I wish to become a master of nothing, but it is hard work.

To expect nothing, to seek nothing, to be nothing calls for special equipment. Some, I inherited from my grandfather: a sturdy wish-rope with a hook at the end. This is used to grab onto mythical embankments, edges of momentary but promising madness, shorelines of clouds that border unseen countries. The user is required to have strong arms: first the rope is twirled quickly, around and around, until it makes a roaring sound, and then flicked upward with hope and despair. If the throw is true, the rope remains suspended in air, its grappling end invisible high in the sky. Then you begin to climb. My grandfather threw this rope one day and climbed and was never seen again, but he was considerate enough to unhook the rope from wherever it had grabbed and throw it down to earth again. It was kept in the basement until I found it, coiled like a wise snake, ready for the world.

Another thing you will need is a small notebook and a pencil. I especially like the short stubby pencils given to people who play golf. They are never too sharp; kept in your pocket, they do not pierce the pocket and dock themselves squarely in your thigh, leaving a little black mark from the lead when you pull it out.

This small notebook and pencil must never be used. The temptation here is quite great, but a little note here, a piece of poetry there, and before you know it, you are reflecting upon your experiences. It is a little known fact, but these experiences when reflected upon turn to dust, and you end up walking on them without knowing they were once alive.

Finally, each traveler must have sturdy shoes that once belonged to a close friend. This is important: these shoes must be indispensable (you must give away all of your own shoes to other friends...), and you must wear them all of the time. You must allow yourself to feel how they do not fit just right, and while not painful, how they are always thinking of someone else's feet; someone else's arch vaulting upward; someone else's toes. This will help you remember that you are not the only one walking around, trying to become a master of nothing. You will also smile as you remember your friend, and wonder whether he is barefoot now, walking on the

snows of some mythical peak, his feet cold or warm
with dreams.

The other things you need you will have to discover
for yourself. I used to have a manual here, but I've
misplaced it. That is OK: It leaves me nothing to go
on, and increasingly, that's the way I like it.

8.

Sometimes our parents come to us out of the blue. Some of us grew up in a dark tunnel. Some grew up in apple orchards. Some grew up at home and some on the road between places. Sometimes our parents were not our parents: They were a tunnel through which we entered this world and they were confused conduits, unsure of themselves, mirrored in a crazy world, unable to talk.

Often, we spent the first part of our lives with hammers and chisels, trying to shape parents from our parents who were not our parents. This exercise sometimes works, but everyone is wounded in the process of inserting nails and screws, tying one part to another.

But because God is kind and cannot be otherwise, our real parent keeps searching for us all through our childhood. We sometimes hear their calling in our hearts and our ears hear a kind of whispery buzz. We hear this sound in water, in air, in anything flowing.

These volunteers don't know who we are and we don't know they are waiting, but they are. And then, when conditions are right, they appear. And though it seems like it is a meeting for the first time, all the people involved seem to know each other and tilt their heads, listening to this ripple that begins to become a roar. Everybody wonders, "Who is this person?"

God asks only one thing of us: To keep looking. Eventually, we find ourselves.

9.

I was born in a beach house. I was born on the
tundra, in a small village near a coal-stack, on a
street near a canal, in a place that was Irish, that
was Jewish, that was German, a place that had a
priest and a grandmother. Both spoke Polish and
had legs and dresses and talked in black and white.

I was born with parents, with walking confusions,
with puddles, with oil on the tops of puddles. My
parents were poor, poor in understanding, in
temperament, in capacity, in music.

I was therefore born without parents, nothing on
the clipboard, no interference thrown between me
and the plain. I was born in a tunnel, in a nuance, in
a system, in a box, in a sieve, in an emergency, in a
quarantine.

Which is to say that one day one of my real parents
came out of the blue. This didn't happen all at once.
No. We had been searching for each other for some
time but didn't know it. We had heard each other's
voice in childhood but didn't pay attention.
Naturally, we both liked music.

Because of my severe loss of a memory I never had,
I could not approach this new father or find this
new mother easily. I had to fight my way to the

shoulder of the road I was on and let every truck I was driving pass me by.

I had to get out of the car, unhitch the horse, put the mule out to pasture and walk. Then I had to walk slowly enough so that the one who was ahead of me on the road, the one who had to get out of his own carriage and cradle and town and book, could see me as I found him.

He was soft-armed plenty and had tallness instead of hate.

God is infinitely kind.

10.

Bones in the graveyard cannot embrace. Instead they lie there thinking, waiting for the kindness of the living to lay them out straight, to ease their cramps away, to flick away dust or earth, to honor them or love them or soothe them or sing to them.

I remember when I was alive someone said something nice to me and I remained like a skeleton, isolated in my grave, as wave upon wave of life washed over me. I was not ready for a mouth to suck the nectar in; I was not ready for arms that could reach out and touch the one who sent me that love note, I was not ready to have a beating torso, pulsing genitals, or stamping feet, hot with dance. But that was years ago, and little by little I got younger.

Flesh filled out my face. I grew a beard. My arms arose, my fingers gained rings. My heart thumped and my pelvis softened and moved like something in a cradle. It was when I learned to walk that I left the grave and found the Other, in people, in leaves and trees, and in the singing that entered my now-ready, bud-like ears.

11.

I had a dream: I was in an immense auditorium
under a dark dome where all the sick people were
being entertained. That sweet smell of cancer-death
was everywhere. Some people were walking with
escorts, some with friends. Some were lying in
hospital beds. It was clear the concert was about to
start.

I was with a friend who was excited and happy to be
there, and although I was the one with her, she
didn't seem to need me: she had other friends and
family there, and she talked to them in hoarse,
excited whispers.

Where is this Place, O God? And how in your
kindness did you bring it to us? And after the
concert, do we get to speak to the musicians, who I
see moving around, setting up their chairs, wearing
evening dress?

The whole dome was hushed with anticipation and
filled with chatter at the same time. The stars were
out, but we were inside. It was gray and it was
beautiful and people walked up and down the stairs,
finding their way.

12.

I have finally begun to like what I like, with no apologies to myself or others. "I like this crappy soda, this cloudy day, this silly music, this touch right here, this kiss in the middle of the street."

I have finally begun liking to pray this way, with shouts or silence, in a book or in a stone. Where have all my taunters gone? They have dissolved into ash, burned away into the remains of what is burned.

Now, when I like something, I like you, I like me. I always mention God, because I like Him too, and I always think of what I can do to help others because I like that too, and I always smile, with what I like dripping down the sides of my mouth, a little surprised to be talked to while I'm eating...

13.

Something goes out of our house, out of our bed,
out of our body. We begin to say goodbye to it,
farewell! Adios! It leaves, not looking back because
it has somewhere to go, something to do. Then we
tap it on the shoulder, just before it turns the corner
and say to it, as it looks back over its shoulder,
"Why don't you consider changing this?" or
"Remember what I told you!" or "Do you really
think you should be leaving quite so soon?"

O son of man, O daughter of woman! The shadow
of the Gate is unbearable. The thought that night
will fall unthinkable and yet we think it. And if we
let them leave...! O, it will leave a mark on our soul,
the red stripe of a whip on our flesh...

Every leaving is a little death, a little incursion of
the dark (we feel) into the Light of our life. But I
say: Let it go, and it will send letters home,
messages of victory, sonnets of Love. This is how we
move the Darkness back: by living and saying
goodbye, our waving hands the hieroglyphics of
Light.

14.

Look at your lover's face! Do not think of your
beloved as being present only and only now, the age
they are, the who they are, the what. This person in
front of you is all of their time. They are wide-eyed
five and soft-boned one, and running three and
smoothed-skinned, moist-haired seven, they are
eleven, sneaking new dreams into the world and
teenagers and young men and women. Can you see
it in their shining? Do not look at them as "your
love," "your husband," "your wife." Right now your
lover is someone who never knew you but looked
for you, someone who anticipated love with
mouthfuls of rain, staring into a storm, laughing,
but didn't expect you to be the one who came,
falling, into their hearts. And if you are having
trouble with them, it is because you both have
forgotten who you both are, all of these people in
one moment, no past, no future, just the intense
scintillation of a million moments of history,
happening in the eyes of the one you stare at with
longing. Be surprised.

15.

The body of an angel is its message. The arms of an angel are its message. Its breathing is its message, likewise its thighs, its thoughts and feelings.

When we talk about an angel we think of a being who contains a message, an action, a thought or a feeling, but it is not so.

The higher an angel, the more it is fully its message with nothing left over for something extra. No loose robe flapping, no sandals walking, no air pumped around its shoulders by wings.

This is usually incomprehensible to human beings who are containers that hold various things. In this way we are holding things and losing things and summoning things up and pushing things down.

When we no longer contain God within ourselves, when "ourselves" is something that has shattered irrevocably, when there is no longer a difference between what is inside and what is outside, then we are like angels, a song ourselves, grateful to have one urge, one mission, one life.

16.

The day after we make a sound it is silent.

Then the day when we make a sound falls silent and we are surprised to see the words turn into mist as they leave our mouths.

Then the moment before we speak turns into nothing.

You would think that we would get the message and stop, but we don't. Even then we have something to say, something about silence, something about compassion or the posture of generosity, something about something.

If we pray hard enough during these moments, if we are lucky, our brains begin disintegrating and we forget about the mist of words rumbling around in our mouths, and it is our ears that fall silent, and everything we say, we miss. People tell us later what we said and we say, "Really? Did I say that?" and we either applaud or cry, depending upon the words we hear them say.

17.

I brought a tree home to dinner one night who proved to be quite a conversationalist. First the soup was brought to the table. I dug in right away. The tree demurred. Did not pick up the spoon, did not sniff the air above the plate, in fact, did nothing. I was ashamed and realized I had jumped the gun; that I had shamelessly let my greed get the better of me, forgetting about my guests. After the soup we had meat and vegetables. This time I waited for the tree to eat, but the tree did not. I waited and waited and in the waiting I learned something. I learned about the power of silence and waiting. At first, I thought of these two things as powerful lessons that would lead me somewhere, but after more waiting and more silence, I began to see that they led nowhere, and in fact were nothing and changed nothing. They were completely pristine. This taught me something profound, and I began to look at the world in a new, pristine way. Everything seemed fresh and new. I bowed to the tree, but the tree refused to take my accolades and I saw even then the tree was teaching me, not allowing me to get away with anything. It did not need my accolades or my condolences: it was itself and only itself. In time, living with this tree in my house, I put down roots myself and began to accrue nourishment right from where I was. When guests would come to dinner,

smiling, I would watch them eat, a leafy sparkle in
my eye.

18.

Old dog lying in the sun.

The sense of smell less than it was.

Old dog knows where the sunlight is in summer, where the stove is in winter, watches everything. Enlightenment watches all entanglements, gets caught by the briars but is not their prisoner. Slips by in dreamtime, rescues nobody and everybody at the same time.

Awakening is filled with flash. It lets you know the sun has risen. Old dog just raises his head, plops it down again and sleeps. Awakening has a song, a beautiful song. Old dog has only a piece of theme and a little rhythm: all the melody has meandered away. He hears other people singing it and is glad to listen. It fills him with happiness.

Awakening posts messages on every electric utility pole: it advertises the good news. It is important to write down awakening's telephone number and get in touch as soon as you can. Enlightenment forgot to charge the cell phone, but you can find him shopping at the supermarket: one bag of onions and some lentils for Lebanese soup.

Oh people! God is in the wind above the house.
God is crying in the branches, listen! Please awaken
and then go further. Forget about it all.